ISSUES THAT CONCERN YOU

Homelessness

Arthur Gillard, *Book Editor*

9/12

GREENHAVEN PRESS

A part of Gale, Cengage Learning

GALE
CENGAGE Learning

Detroit • New York • San Francisco • New Haven, Conn • Waterville, Maine • London

Elizabeth Des Chenes, *Managing Editor*

© 2012 Greenhaven Press, a part of Gale, Cengage Learning

Gale and Greenhaven Press are registered trademarks used herein under license.

For more information, contact:
Greenhaven Press
27500 Drake Rd.
Farmington Hills, MI 48331-3535
Or you can visit our Internet site at gale.cengage.com

For product information and technology assistance, contact us at

Gale Customer Support, 1-800-877-4253
For permission to use material from this text or product, submit all requests online at www.cengage.com/permissions

Further permissions questions can be e-mailed to permissionrequest@cengage.com

Articles in Greenhaven Press anthologies are often edited for length to meet page requirements. In addition, original titles of these works are changed to clearly present the main thesis and to explicitly indicate the author's opinion. Every effort is made to ensure that Greenhaven Press accurately reflects the original intent of the authors. Every effort has been made to trace the owners of copyrighted material.

Cover image © George P. Choma/Shutterstock.com.

LIBRARY OF CONGRESS CATALOGING-IN-PUBLICATION DATA

Homelessness / Arthur Gillard, book editor.
   p. cm. -- (Issues that concern you)
 Includes bibliographical references and index.
 ISBN 978-0-7377-5694-4 (hardcover)
1. Homelessness--United States. 2. Homeless persons--United States. I. Gillard, Arthur.
 HV4505.H65527 2012
 362.50973--dc23
                         2011041396

Printed in the United States of America
1 2 3 4 5 6 7 16 15 14 13 12

CONTENTS

INTRODUCTION

Often when people think of the homeless, they picture an addict begging for money or a mentally unstable person muttering on a street corner. It is true that the rates of mental illness and substance abuse among the homeless are much higher than average. According to the National Alliance to End Homelessness, "About 25 percent of the homeless population has serious mental illness, including chronic depression, bipolar disorder, and schizophrenia . . . 46 percent of homeless respondents reported having an alcohol use problem in the past year, and 38 percent reported a problem with drug use in the past year."[1] However, there is no "typical" homeless person. The homeless population is diverse, comprised of many different people from all walks of life.

Nor are the homeless always living on the street. As Karen Kasland writes in *Current Health 2*, "If you think homeless people live on the streets, you're only partly right. As defined in the Homeless Assistance Act, a federal law, families are considered homeless if they are living in shelters, cars, campgrounds, abandoned buildings, trailer parks, and motels. Also included are families 'doubling up' with other people because they've lost their own places."[2]

There are many ways people can become homeless. As mentioned above, mental illness and drug addiction are factors for some. In other cases domestic violence plays a role; many women who are beaten by their husbands and live in poverty face a difficult choice between staying in the abusive relationship or becoming homeless. Other factors include declining public assistance, reduced work opportunities, increases in poverty, and lack of medical care, all of which put pressure on individuals and families, causing some to slip into homelessness.

No matter the reason, losing one's home is a very disorienting experience. Carly remembers her first night as a homeless teen: "It was the worst night of my life: I was sitting under a playground slide, hiding from the cops, or anyone, who might see me and turn me in. I kept looking and listening in every direction—terrified that I'd get caught, anxious about how I'd get through another night like this, and so ashamed of my life. I was 16—and homeless. I kept asking myself, What did I do to deserve this?"[3]

Carly's troubles started when she was eight and her mother was diagnosed with cancer and lupus. Her father was not allowed to be around his children due to legal trouble. But this challenging family background was only a prelude to what happened next. When Carly was sixteen her mother died, after which her older sister Kate started taking care of her. They fought constantly, however, and her sister would sometimes get violent, pushing or hitting her. When the violence escalated one night to Kate choking her, Carly knew she had to leave right away for her own safety. For the next six months, Carly slept in cars, on the street, or stayed with friends, hiding the fact that she was homeless the whole time—until, fortunately for her, a school administrator discovered her secret and helped her to get off the streets.

Public concern about homelessness has waxed and waned over the years. The highest period of interest to date may have been during the 1980s. In 1981 the United Nations declared that 1987 would be the International Year of Shelter for the Homeless. In the United States, a number of events were held to support the homeless and bring attention to the issue. Most notable was the "Hands Across America" fundraiser in 1986, in which over 6 million people held hands to form a chain 4,152 miles long that spanned the entire country, from New York City to Long Beach, California, with the goal of raising awareness and money to help the homeless and hungry. Interest in the issue gradually declined through the 1990s and into the twenty-first century. But in the past few years concern with homelessness appears to be on the rise again due to the severe recession that started in 2007, which has resulted in significant increases in unemployment, poverty, and loss of homes to foreclosure—all of which are known precursors to homelessness. In January 2008 a Gallup poll found that 38 percent of Americans worried about hunger and homelessness a great deal, and 35 percent worried about it a fair amount.[4]

No matter what the circumstances, being homeless can be the most debilitating and traumatic experience of a person's life.

Mark Horvath, who has himself experienced homelessness, suggests considering what it is like to be suddenly homeless: "Sadly, thousands of people experience their first night [of] homelessness each year. No matter what circumstances led to their homelessness—eviction, foreclosure, unemployment, addiction, mental illness, domestic violence—being homeless for that first night is painful. Now imagine a personal crisis has hit, and you no longer have access to money or a place to stay. It is now your first night homeless. What would you do?"[5]

Authors in this anthology offer a variety of perspectives on homelessness. In addition, the volume contains a thorough bibliography, a list of organizations to contact for further information, and appendixes to help the reader understand and explore the topic. The appendix titled "What You Should Know About Homelessness" offers facts about the problem. The appendix "What You Should Do About Homelessness" offers advice for young people who are concerned with this issue. With all these features, *Issues That Concern You: Homelessness* provides an excellent resource for everyone interested in this topic.

Notes

1. National Alliance to End Homelessness, "Issues: Mental/Physical Health." www.endhomelessness.org/section/issues/mental_ physical_health.

2. Karen Kasland, "Out of Place: For Homeless Teens, Challenges Are Everywhere," *Current Health 2*, March 2010, pp. 26+.

3. Jessica Press, "'I Was Homeless and No One Knew': Carly, 20, Had a Childhood Just Like Everyone Else's. So How Did She End Up Living on the Streets?," *Seventeen*, April 2009, pp. 108+.

4. "Poverty in the United States," in *Social Welfare: Fighting Poverty and Homelessness*, ed. Melissa J. Doak. Detroit: Gale, Cengage Learning, 2010.

5. Mark Horvath, "My First Night Homeless: A True Story," *Huffington Post*, April 20, 2011. www.huffingtonpost.com/mark -horvath/my-first-night-homeless_b_850145.html.

ONE

An Overview of Homelessness

Gale Group

The following viewpoint, provided by the Gale Group's *Student Resource Center*, gives an overview of the problem of homelessness. According to the author, homelessness is a complex issue that varies by region and culture. For example, in the United States the largest number of homeless people are middle-aged men, whereas globally most homeless people are women and their dependent children. The author notes that many different factors can result in homelessness, including natural disasters (such as Hurricane Katrina in 2005), war, ethnic violence, and urban development and industrialization. The Gale Group contends that globally, homelessness is caused mainly by poverty, but it also cites research that found a high correlation between US homelessness and disabilities such as mental illness and addiction to alcohol or other drugs.

A homeless person is someone who is unable to secure and maintain a permanent, safe, and adequate dwelling. Homelessness is the condition of being homeless, and it represents a broad social category of people who are, for any number of reasons, left without a place to call their own.

The subject of homeless persons is a complex one, owing to the various categories of people and the circumstances that led to their becoming homeless. The scope and severity of the problem also varies by region and culture: in the United States, for example, the highest proportion of homeless people are middle-aged men. Globally, however, the vast majority of homeless people are women, many with dependent children.

Homeless people face a variety of challenges, including lack of personal safety and hygiene. Most have no place to secure their possessions and are under constant threat of theft and violence. For many in Europe and North America, there is limited access to health care and education; in other parts of the world, access to these resources is virtually nonexistent. For many, there is little or no connection with family or friends, and almost all homeless people must suffer the stigma and abuse that accompanies their social status.

Causes of Homelessness

Actual statistics on the number and condition of homeless people are notoriously difficult to obtain, especially in countries outside North America and Europe. At one point during the late 1990s, the United Nations [U.N.] estimated that as many as one hundred million people were homeless. More recently, in the United States, the National Law Center on Homelessness and Poverty estimates that more than three million people "experience" homelessness in any given year.

How one defines "homeless" also determines who gets counted. In the United States, the McKinney-Vento Homeless Assistance Act of 1987 defined a homeless person as one who "lacks a fixed, regular, and adequate nighttime residence or has a primary nighttime residence that is a supervised publicly operated shelter . . . temporary residence . . . [or] public or private place not ordinarily used as regular sleeping accommodations for human beings." The United Nations' Centre for Human Settlements, which focuses on matters related to habitat and urban development, has attempted to include those living in substandard and temporary housing,

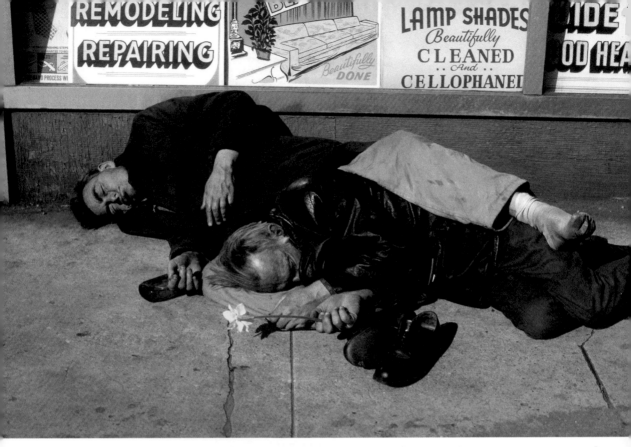

In the United States the highest proportion of homeless people are middle-aged men; however, globally, the vast majority are women and children.

but it acknowledges that the definition of homeless can vary by region and culture, and that attempting to apply an international standard may, in certain circumstances, define as homeless those who might not otherwise consider themselves as such.

Homelessness stems from a variety of cultural, political, and economic factors. In many parts of the world, entire communities of people become homeless as the result of war, insurrection, or ethnic violence. Industrialization and urban development can have a profound effect on the poor and disadvantaged and often leads to the impoverishment of large segments of the population. Natural disasters, such as the Indonesian tsunamis of 2004, or Hurricane Katrina in 2005, can swell the ranks of homeless people in a matter of days.

In some parts of the world, women have no property rights; those unaffiliated with a husband or family must often fend for themselves and their children. As more and more urban settings undergo renewal and growth, the influx of wealth can drive the value of certain properties beyond the means of those already living there, resulting in forced evictions and destruction of property.

Poverty and Homelessness

Globally, homelessness is caused mainly by poverty. The fastest growing segment of impoverished people are women and young girls, resulting in what many have called the global feminization of poverty. Women are less likely to be employed and able to obtain loans for housing and are much more likely to be among the refugee populations caused by civil wars or other internal

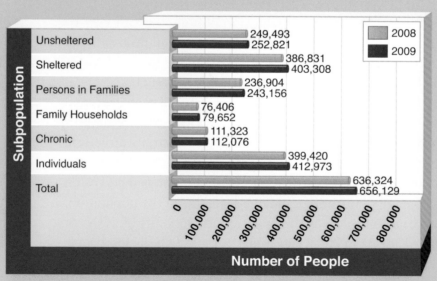

People in America Experiencing Homelessness by Subpopulation, 2008 to 2009

Subpopulation	2008	2009
Unsheltered	249,493	252,821
Sheltered	386,831	403,308
Persons in Families	236,904	243,156
Family Households	76,406	79,652
Chronic	111,323	112,076
Individuals	399,420	412,973
Total	636,324	656,129

Taken from: M. William Sermons and Peter Witte, "State of Homelessness in America January 2011: A Research Report on Homelessness," National Alliance to End Homelessness, January 11, 2011. www.endhomelessness.org /content/article/detail/3668.

conflicts. Thus, women, along with so many of their children, have become disproportionately represented among the world's homeless population.

In Europe and North America, where more detailed research and analyses of homeless populations have been conducted, the correlation of poverty and homelessness has also been well established. However, researchers have also determined that many homeless people suffer from a variety of disabilities, such as mental illness, drug or alcohol addiction, or other vulnerabilities that render the individual unfit or unable to obtain or maintain their own domicile. In the United States, during the 1960s and 1970s, mental health professionals advocated the mass deinstitutionalization of patients from state mental hospitals. But without facilities for treating these patients, many were left to wander the streets untreated and uncared for.

In the United States, as in Europe, determining the causes of homelessness has become a politically charged affair. Many point to various economic and social policies of the 1980s, and the administration of then-President Ronald Reagan, that were hostile to the poor and disadvantaged, such as cuts in funding for welfare programs and low-income housing assistance. Others charge that the transformation of the nation's industrial economy to a lower-paying service economy put added pressure on those already at the bottom rungs of the socioeconomic ladder. Urban renewal, and the replacement of affordable housing with more expensive and exclusive housing projects, has also been cited as a contributing factor.

Increased industrialization, brought about by economic globalization, has resulted in a mass migration of laborers from poor, rural communities to richer and more densely populated city centers. This rapid "urbanization" has created huge social and economic disparities. Though not everyone living below the poverty line is homeless, those with little or no income represent the highest category of risk for becoming homeless. Children who are forced to live and beg on the streets are especially vulnerable to exploitation and violence.

Responses to Homelessness

Most modern industrialized nations provide some form of govern-ment assistance either directly or through agencies organized to help homeless people in their communities. In the United States, many of these are religion-based organizations, which began receiving federal support during the George W. Bush adminis-tration of 2001–2009. Others, such as the National Law Center on Homelessness and Poverty, provide litigation, advocacy, and educational services to programs that seek to alleviate homeless-ness. The National Coalition for the Homeless has created a national network of activists, community, and faith-based service providers whose aim is to end homelessness by not only providing for the needs of the homeless, but raising public awareness and advocating social changes needed to prevent homelessness. The National Alliance to End Homelessness is a federation of service providers and public agencies dedicated to research, education, and community-planning projects aimed at ending homelessness.

The United Nations Human Settlements Programme is man-dated by the U.N. General Assembly to "promote socially and environmentally sustainable towns and cities with the goal of pro-viding adequate shelter for all." In its 1996 Istanbul Declaration on Human Settlements, the agency acknowledges the deteriora-tion of living standards in many large cities around the world and proposes to achieve its ends by improving the quality of life through the eradication of poverty and discrimination, promotion of human rights, and the provisioning of education and health care services.

TWO

Tent Cities Can Help Solve the Homelessness Problem

Hubert G. Locke

Hubert G. Locke of Seattle is professor and dean emeritus of the University of Washington's Evans School of Public Affairs. In the following viewpoint Locke describes the tent city that his church allowed over eighty homeless people to set up on its parking lot. He argues that although it is not an ideal solution, the tent city is helping the people who live there to have temporary shelter and relative safety. According to Locke, in official shelters families are often separated, with adults and children required to stay in separate areas. In the tent city, on the other hand, families are able to stay together. Locke says that permitting the tent city to operate is a way to help homeless people immediately, while longer-term solutions are pursued by the various agencies tasked with helping the homeless.

The problem of homelessness has taken on a personal dimension for me during the past six weeks. I'm a member of the church (University Christian) where Tent City has been encamped in the church parking lot since Oct. 10 [2008].

It all took place, albeit rather hurriedly, at the invitation of congregation leaders; a few feathers were ruffled in the process because the church is fiercely democratic, very much used to making major decisions as a body. By far, the larger problem has been confronting the reality of 80-plus people, trying to live their lives huddled under canvass and sleeping on asphalt where we are accustomed to parking our cars on Sunday and other occasions, as well as enjoying the income the lot provides during the week.

At a congregational meeting last Sunday, the church treasurer dutifully calculated the loss in income from parking fees, as well as the lot's unavailability for weddings, musicals and other events. The treasurer, however, was among the first to dismiss those factors as significant and in the ensuing discussion, "revenue loss" was not mentioned again. The principal difficulty the congregation faces is that under city ordinance, the encampment is illegal and the church is subject to a rather hefty fine if it permits Tent City to continue occupying its parking area.

Making the city the villain in this saga has become easy for some. Tent City has been derisively dubbed "Nickelsville" and municipal bureaucrats depicted as cold-hearted in a situation that calls for compassion. Church officials, however, report that the city—including the Mayor's Office—is working cooperatively with the congregation to try to find an acceptable solution.

The city's position is not only that municipal ordinances forbid such temporary settlements; the arrangement is also unsafe and unsanitary. The city has a point. There are no bathing facilities and Porta-Potties serve as the only available lavatories. As the weather worsens, the risk of a fire from whatever heating devices are being used becomes all the greater. Besides, says the city, shelters for the homeless are provided all across Seattle.

The homeless note, in response, that shelters—however well-meaning their providers—are frightfully demeaning places where one must spend the night on floor mats or cots, within arms reach of total strangers. Many shelters have restrictions of one sort or another so that adults must be housed separately from children, with the result that families are broken up in the process of trying to find a place to spend the night. Tent City, according to its spokespeople, has become a community of sorts in which its inhabitants help and support one another; 16 of its 80-plus inhab-

Change in Unsheltered Homeless Population by State from 2008–2009

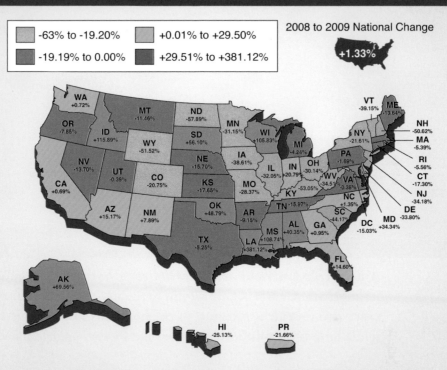

Unsheltered Homeless Percent Change, 2008 to 2009

Legend:
- -63% to -19.20%
- -19.19% to 0.00%
- +0.01% to +29.50%
- +29.51% to +381.12%

2008 to 2009 National Change
+1.33%

WA +0.72%
MT -11.46%
ND -57.89%
MN -31.15%
VT -39.15%
ME -13.64%
OR -7.85%
ID +115.89%
WY -51.52%
SD +56.10%
WI +105.83%
NY -21.61%
NH -50.62%
MA -5.39%
NV -13.70%
UT -0.39%
CO -20.75%
NE -15.70%
IA -38.61%
MI -4.24%
PA -1.69%
RI -5.56%
CA +0.69%
IL -32.05%
IN -20.79%
OH -30.14%
WV -34.51%
VA -0.35%
CT -17.30%
NJ -34.18%
KS -17.65%
MO -28.37%
KY -53.05%
AZ +15.17%
NM +7.89%
OK +48.79%
AR -9.15%
TN -15.97%
NC +1.35%
DE -33.80%
MD +34.34%
SC -44.17%
DC -15.03%
TX -5.25%
MS -108.74%
AL +40.35%
GA +0.95%
LA +381.12%
FL +14.60%
AK +69.56%
HI -25.13%
PR -21.66%

Taken from: M. William Sermons and Peter Witte, "State of Homelessness in America January 2011: A Research Report on Homelessness," National Alliance to End Homeless, January 11, 2011, p. 14. www.endhomelessness.org/content/article/detail/3668.

itants have managed to find work or more permanent housing since it's been ensconced at the church.

No one is under the illusion that a Tent City is other than a temporary answer to a long-term question. And the question of homelessness is not one that the city of Seattle can solve by itself. To its credit, Seattle has joined with 20 other metropolitan-area municipalities in pledging support for a Ten-Year Plan to End Homelessness. More than 200 institutions, organizations and agencies are co-signers to the plan—most are churches, mosques

A homeless American war veteran rests in the New Life Evangelistic Center's tent city in St. Louis, Missouri. Tent cities can provide assistance to the homeless in the short term, while long-term solutions are pursued by various agencies.

and synagogues, but they also include the United Way of King County, the state Departments of Corrections and Social and Health Services, the Gates Foundation and Harborview Medical Center.

But the problem is far greater than even this impressive list can address. It is staunchly denied by many experts in the field that a community's efforts to address homelessness have a magnet effect (i.e., word gets out that a given community tries to deal compassionately with the problem and the homeless are accordingly drawn to that community). At the same time, at least one community in Colorado is reputed to be solving its problem by buying one-way bus tickets for its homeless populace to a city in California.

The bottom line is that we are a free country, with no way of sealing municipal or state borders from anyone who wants to migrate to a new place of residence. Individual or even statewide efforts to solve homelessness therefore will get nowhere; what we face is a national dilemma that only a carefully thought-out federal policy and resources can successfully address. One hates to add to the list of imponderables that our president-elect faces, but this is one that—in light of the current economic collapse and its anticipated long-term effects—can only get worse.

THREE

Housing First Approaches Are the Best Solution to Homelessness

Iain Atherton and Carol McNaughton Nicholls

Iain Atherton is a lecturer in nursing at the University of Stirling in Scotland. Carol McNaughton Nicholls is research director of the Health and Wellbeing team at the National Center for Social Research in London, England, and the author of *Transitions Through Homelessness*. In the following viewpoint Atherton and Nicholls argue that the Housing First approach to homelessness has been highly successful in addressing the needs of homeless people. In this model the homeless are provided with independent housing first, and offered optional access to support services. In contrast, a Continuum of Care model requires homeless people to go through treatment programs first, and they are only given access to housing if certain requirements are met. The authors say that over 80 percent of the clients in one Housing First study retained housing during a two-year period, and note that this kind of program reduces costs associated with supporting the homeless population.

Iain Atherton and Carol McNaughton Nicholls, "'Housing First' as a Means of Addressing Multiple Needs and Homelessness," *European Journal of Homelessness*, December 2008, vol. 2. Copyright © 2008 by European Journal of Homelessness. All rights reserved. Reproduced by permission.

The *Housing First* approach has become synonymous with the work of the 'Pathways to Housing', agency, based in New York and operating since 1992. 'Pathways' was set up by a psychologist, Sam Tsemberis, as a response to the problems he saw facing mentally ill patients who had no alternative housing options other than to access shelters or live on the street.

In the *Housing First* approach, access to an independent tenancy comes first. A considerable amount of support is then available to clients. They do not have to accept this assistance, although it is 'assertively provided', in other words, there is considerable encouragement for clients to engage. However, refusal to use treatment services, a relapse, or other problems will not lead to eviction. Clients can be moved to other 'Pathways' apartments if problems develop; this can happen several times if necessary, the ultimate aim being to ensure that housed status is maintained. Only violence towards staff would lead to termination of the client's programme involvement. Tenancies are found in apartment blocks in which no more than 15% of other residents are programme clients, hence getting away from institutionalised accommodation. For the clients, choice is a central component. They choose their apartment, furnishings, the location and times of contact with support workers, and so on. The apartments are privately rented, but 'Pathways' holds the leases and manages the properties. Clients are viewed as being capable of remaining stably housed even if they have serious mental health issues or are misusing drugs.

In contrast, *Continuum of Care* approaches highlight 'treatment first' and the need for a phased 'staircase of transition' to deal with individual problems and needs, leading eventually to resettlement in a secure tenure. Social workers assist clients throughout the process, with progression to the next stage only occurring if and when capacities, such as successfully addressing drug misusing behaviour, are demonstrated. Housing becomes an end goal to be achieved rather than a component in a person's recovery. . . .

Considering the Effectiveness of *Housing First*

North American experience suggests that people with multiple problems, including drug misuse and mental illness, can maintain stable tenancies even if their other problems remain unresolved. Tsemberis *et al.* report that clients randomly allocated to *Housing First* had around an 80% retention rate in housing over a two-year period. As Tsemberis *et al.* point out, such a success rate represents a serious challenge to ideas that hold mentally ill or drug-using individuals to be incapable of maintaining their own tenancy. They found that the degree of residential stability was significantly greater than for those in a *Continuum of Care* control group. Similar and supporting evidence comes from a recent survey by 'Streets to Homes', a project in Toronto, Canada, which also employs a *Housing First* approach that found some 90% of clients still in stable housing one year after being housed. Of those still in stable accommodation, 85% perceived ongoing tenure to be secure and believed themselves to have a positive future.

Notably, the success of the *Housing First* has in no way been the result of less challenging clients being targeted. The programmes in the US have, so far, been aimed only at the chronically homeless who have particularly problematic health and social support needs. These clients are randomly enrolled on *Housing First* programmes on a 'first come first served' basis or selected because they have repeatedly failed to work through a *Continuum of Care* and would not engage with mainstream support services. They are not therefore 'cherry picked' on the basis of 'housing readiness' but rather the opposite, which makes the apparent success of *Housing First* programmes all the more remarkable.

Not only is successful maintenance of a tenancy more likely amongst *Housing First* clients, but health and well-being also seem to benefit. Compared with a comparison group of *Continuum of Care* clients, the *Housing First* tenants had fewer psychiatric admissions, lower emergency admissions, fewer arrests and—at least for *Streets to Homes'* clients in Toronto—reduced drug use.

Housing First Approaches Cost Less

Providing housing and making available substantial levels of support, suggest that *Housing First* approaches will involve considerable expense. [Researchers D.] Culhane *et al.*, however, have demonstrated that when all costs are taken into account the converse is true. They concluded that homeless mentally ill people in New York used $40,451 of services in a year. This *reduced* by $16,281 when they were provided with supportive housing, mainly due to a decrease in emergency service uptake and arrests. The cost of providing housing and support therefore led to an overall net cost reduction.

Why has *Housing First* achieved such positive outcomes? An important part of the success of the 'Pathways to Housing' project in New York may have been the type of housing which clients occupied. As noted earlier, Pathways' clients were housed in blocks in which no more than 15% of residents were fellow programme participants. This approach is in contrast to other examples of projects which have relied on communal hostels to a

In the Main Street Methodist Church in Nashua, New Hampshire, volunteers organized by Continuum of Care assist the homeless. The organization offers services that includes a phased "staircase transition" to deal with the homeless individual's specific problems.

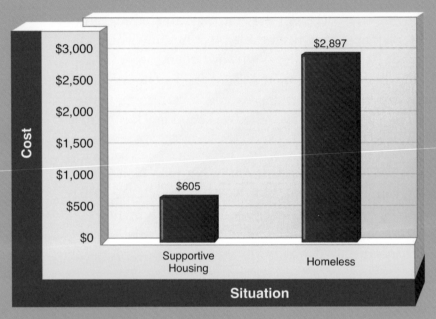

Average Monthly Public Costs for Supportive Housing and Comparable Homeless Persons in Los Angeles

Supportive housing saves the public money. Homeless persons incur increased costs for services, such as hospital visits, inpatient and outpatient clinics, mental health services and food stamps.

Taken from: Daniel Flaming, Michael Matsunaga and Patrick Burns, "Where We Sleep: The Costs of Housing and Homelessness in Los Angeles," Los Angeles, November 2009. www.economicrt.org/summaries/Where_We_Sleep.html.

greater extent. Hostels have been recognised as an environment in which people are brought into contact with others who are misusing drugs; hardly conducive to reducing or ceasing drug use or treatment of mental illness. Not all clients in the Toronto 'Streets to Homes' *Housing First* programme had their own tenancy, some residing in hostels. The client survey, however, noted that those living independently perceived themselves to be happier with their housing situation. Having an independent tenancy is a component of well-being in its own right, which is an important part of motivating people to take control of their own lives.

The provision of assertive services is likely to have significantly contributed to helping people maintain their tenancy and to address their social and health problems. The New York and Toronto programmes consist of sizeable support teams, including nurses, psychiatrists, drug misuse councillors and peer supporters. Clients of the 'Pathways to Housing' project in New York, however, were found to use services *less* than those in the *Continuum of Care* control group. Such a result is not surprising, given that maintaining or achieving housing status was not predicated on service engagement. Furthermore, it has also been suggested that the integrated nature of the services offered by Pathways' teams explains their clients' lower contact with services—they holistically received support and housing through one integrated package and did not require contact with other services.

The combination of early housing and readily available, integrated social and health care support may explain the success of *Housing First*; the two components interact to produce improved outcomes. However, it has long been recognised that an effective homelessness policy requires both components.

FOUR

Housing First Approaches Are Not a Long-Term Solution to Homelessness

Ralph da Costa Nunez

Ralph da Costa Nunez has served as president of the Institute for Children, Poverty, and Homelessness since the organization's founding in 1990 and is also president and chief executive officer of Homes for the Homeless, a leading social services agency. He has a PhD in political science from Columbia University. In the following viewpoint Nunez claims that the Housing First strategy has only been successful for a small subset of the homeless population. According to Nunez, when the program was expanded to cover all homeless families with children, significant problems began to show up. He says that program costs have increased dramatically, and the rate of recidivism (people returning to homelessness) has also shown large increases. Nunez argues that the initial limited success of the Housing First principle was not replicated when it was more generally applied, and that more study is needed to find the most effective solutions.

Ralph da Costa Nunez, "One Size Does Not Fit All: Rapid Rehousing and Homeless Families," *The Huffington Post*, July 16, 2010. www.huffingtonpost.com. Copyright © 2010 by Institute for Children, Poverty and Homelessness. All rights reserved. Reproduced by permission.

Over the last two decades, rapid rehousing strategies have grown to become the dominant trend among the homeless policy and services community. Yet New York City is emerging as an example of how a narrow focus on housing can have serious unintended consequences for so many homeless families. A June 2010 Institute for Children, Poverty, and Homelessness (ICPH) brief linking aggressive rehousing to recidivism in New York City, *Boomerang Homeless Families*, raises questions as to the efficacy of rapid rehousing in ensuring the long-term self-sufficiency of homeless families.

Rapid rehousing is an iteration of the Housing First strategy, an approach which identifies stable housing as the most pressing need of the homeless and posits that any other needs can be dealt with by accessing mainstream resources afterwards. In contrast, the Continuum of Care approach utilizes an array of housing options and support services designed to move homeless families from emergency shelter to transitional housing to permanent housing and to provide services at each stage. Services offered along the way are intended to help clients achieve housing stability by preparing them for self-sufficiency.

Housing First has been very successful in getting primarily chronically homeless single adults off of the streets, out of emergency shelters, and quickly into permanent housing with access to mainstream services. More recently, this strategy, which was successful for a very specific population, has been applied to homeless families with children. In fact, rapid rehousing was codified into federal law in 2009 with the Homeless Prevention and Rapid Re-housing Program (HPRP), which aims to prevent and mitigate homelessness through rapid rehousing assistance, and the Homeless Emergency Assistance and Rapid Transition to Housing Act (HEARTH), which expressly emphasizes rapid rehousing for homeless families. These funding streams have fundamentally changed the way localities approach family homelessness, yet it remains unclear if the strategy works well for families.

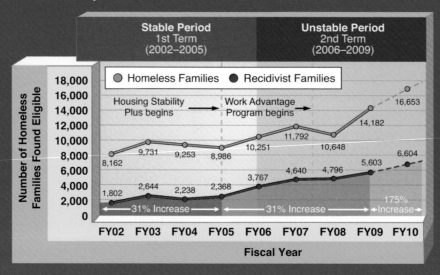

Homeless and Recidivist Families in New York City 2002–2009

Following the introduction of the aggressive rehousing initiative Housing Stability Plus (HSP) in New York City in 2005, the rate of recidivism (families returning to the homeless shelter system after being independently housed for a period of time) increased dramatically.

Taken from: "Boomerang Homeless Families: Aggressive Rehousing Policies in New York City," Institute for Children, Poverty, & Homelessness, June 2010. www.icphusa.org/pdf/reports/icp_Opinion_brief.pdf.

Problems with Rapid Rehousing Approach

Rapid rehousing applies the same Housing First principle to all families, regardless of needs, and despite the fact that the causes of family homelessness are complex and families often face multiple barriers to self-sufficiency. The strategy's short-term focus on housing ignores the multi-faceted realities of these families' lives—relegating adult education, job training, income supports, domestic violence issues, or health problems to secondary importance. Data are beginning to show that rapid rehousing may have serious longer-term consequences for families and family shelter systems.

Boomerang Homeless Families finds that in New York City, the shift to aggressive rehousing in 2005 fueled recidivism: between that year and 2009, the number of families entering shelter increased by 58% while recidivism rose by 137%, and it is projected to reach 179% at the end of this fiscal year. This dramatic increase in recidivism following enactment of aggressive rehousing policies suggests that it was related to immediately moving families from transitional shelters to permanent housing before they were ready and able to retain independent housing through self-sufficiency. These families may not have had access to the services targeted to their specific needs that would have been available to them in shelter.

These policies have been costly to the City; prior to aggressive rehousing, the average cost of recidivism was declining and around $68 million a year—post-aggressive rehousing, the cost rose to about $141 million a year. While rapid rehousing resulted in quickly moving families out of shelter, and thus reducing the shelter census and length of stay, they have not been effective in achieving the long-term goal of permanently transitioning families to self-sufficiency. Clearly, reducing the shelter census should not be the goal—permanent self-sufficiency should be.

It is becoming increasingly clear that aggressive rehousing has failed in New York City, even though the City leadership has the political will to address the problem, a relatively large prevention system, and well-coordinated access to mainstream resources. Given this, there is little to suggest that these aggressive rehousing policies will work in other localities that may lack education, job training, and employment supports and the political commitment to address family homelessness with a comprehensive strategy.

More Research Is Needed

More research is needed to understand why families come back into the shelter system so that we can create interventions to improve self-sufficiency. The rapid rehousing approach should be vigorously evaluated alongside the Continuum of Care approach to examine the long-term impact of these strategies on homeless families. Policymakers should closely monitor the rates at which rapidly rehoused families return to the shelter system and should anticipate that the recent 2009 HPRP and HEARTH funding, which dramatically shifted homeless services towards rapid rehousing, will have unintended consequences. The effects are likely only just beginning to show up in homeless data.

Going forward, it is necessary to examine and track the impact and outcomes of rapid rehousing in a meaningful way—with an eye to individual family needs as well as recidivism rates. While

In New York City between 2005 and 2009, the number of families entering homeless shelters increased by 58 percent, while recidivism rose by 137 percent.

aggressive rehousing may be successful for some families, especially in the short-term, it may not be effective for many homeless families in the long-term. Shelters with targeted services can create "communities of opportunity," which effectively bridge the divide between homelessness and self-sufficiency. As part of a Continuum approach, shelters, when coupled with front-loaded services, can function as an effective tool in reducing family homelessness in the long run.

Lessons we are learning from New York City suggest that the rapid rehousing model should not be blindly replicated, but should instead be rigorously evaluated to better understand whom it works for and whom it does not.

FIVE

Giving Money to Panhandlers Helps the Chronically Homeless

Colorado Springs (CO) Gazette

In the following viewpoint the editorial board of the *Colorado Springs (CO) Gazette* argues that giving money directly to panhandlers is the right thing to do. According to the editors, social services agencies are pressured by the US federal government to make unrealistic plans to end homelessness within ten years in return for federal money. The *Gazette* board says this leads to chronically homeless individuals being seen as enemies of the programs to end homelessness, with the result that shoppers and store owners are strongly discouraged from giving money directly to panhandlers. However, in the *Gazette* editors' opinion, people who are panhandling on the street are often those who have been refused help by every agency that serves the homeless because they are unable or unwilling to follow the rules (such as staying sober). The editors conclude that people should give money directly to panhandlers if they want to help those in greatest need.

Prepare for another organized campaign that says don't give to a person, give only to agencies that are part of a club. Social service agencies from Colorado Springs [CO] and the region revealed a new comprehensive program Monday to address homelessness.

The 10-year-plan is designed to serve every homeless person in the Pikes Peak region, working to help them achieve self-sufficiency. It would focus on medical assistance needs, housing, food, access to a variety of services, veterans' services, emergency services, and assistance with re-entering society from prison or jail.

It's not that social services agencies suddenly developed a new concern for the homeless, at a time when the national and regional economies are in a precarious state. Instead, the agencies are responding to a federal mandate that dictates specific behaviors in return for federal funds.

A woman gives a panhandler money. Many say those who panhandle are often desperate because of the lack of assistance available to them.

The mandates come [from] the U.S. Department of Housing and Urban Development, which decides who does and does not get what are known as Super NOFA (Notice of Funding Availability) funds.

The federal government dangles the funds and tells agencies throughout the country that they will receive money in return for developing plans for "eliminating" homelessness within 10 years. Of course, society will never succeed in eliminating homelessness because millions of homeless Americans would live no other way. To eliminate their chosen or unavoidable lifestyles would involve horrific violations of human rights.

Robert J. Holmes heads Homeward Pikes Peak, an organization that coordinates the efforts of about 50 agencies in the region that help the homeless. Holmes, who worked in school administration for 30 years, seems genuinely devoted to helping those in need. He has a refreshingly realistic view of the government's plan to end homelessness in 10 years.

"I refuse to say we'll end homelessness in 10 years because I can't say something that's not true," Holmes said. "I prefer to say we will give everyone the opportunity to be housed, but not everyone wants that. We will respect that as well."

Social services officials in the region generally agree that the homeless population in Colorado Springs is something close to 2,000. But "homeless" statistics are always a bit misleading, as some people living in the relative lap of luxury—such as those staying long-term on the sofas of wealthy friends—can be counted as "homeless." Holmes said the number of residents who live on the streets of Colorado Springs is between 400 and 500.

Of those, two-thirds are mentally ill and a majority abuse alcohol and/or drugs. Most contemporary street people—those who come to mind when someone says "homeless"—are chronically homeless. Many are likely to live out the rest of their lives on the streets. A great number of street people have been kicked out of every soup kitchen, recovery facility and homeless shelter in town because they simply cannot or will not get sober and follow the rules. Some have mental illnesses, such as schizophrenia or bipolar disorder, which make it nearly impossible for them to play

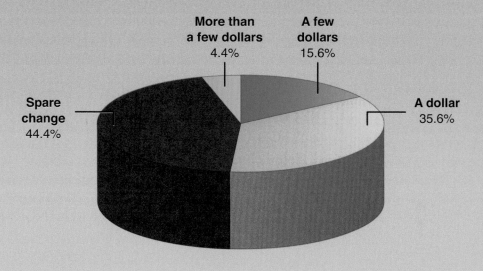

Amount of Money People Give to Panhandlers

More than a few dollars 4.4%

A few dollars 15.6%

Spare change 44.4%

A dollar 35.6%

Taken from: Kim Quintero, "'People think he's just trying to get booze'," April 30, 2009. KVAL.com, www.kval.com/news/44082257.html.

by the rules of conduct social service agencies impose to maintain order. They have fallen through every crack there is, and the unregulated street is all that's left.

Unfortunately, endeavors that fraudulently promise to end homelessness tend to cast the chronically homeless as villains. In Colorado Springs and Denver, for example, HUD-mandated programs to end homelessness have led to campaigns that tell downtown merchants and shoppers to not give handouts.

"I had cards produced so that when panhandlers ask for money, merchants and shoppers can give them a card instead," Holmes said. "One side of the card tells merchants and shoppers not to give to panhandlers, and the other side gives a number the panhandler can call for help. You don't get a lot of 'thank yous' for handing them out."

That's because the chronic street homeless need money, not cards. They are typically vilified by social services professionals in one of two different ways: 1. "They spend the money on alcohol and drugs" and 2. "Some of them get rich."

So what? People who believe that, and don't like it, have the option to walk on by. What these people need least, however, is the federal government urging social service agencies to campaign against their efforts to collect funds on the streets. Considering the fact most of these people have no other viable option for survival, nothing could be more heartless than "don't give" campaigns motivated by federal funding mandates.

Now, to exacerbate well-organized campaigns against panhandlers, City Councilman Jerry Heimlicher has proposed that Colorado Springs use Denver-style feed-the-homeless parking meters. Instead of giving to beggars, who get 100 percent of a donation directly without some agency skimming proceeds, residents will be encouraged to feed special parking meters so Homeward Pikes Peak can dole it out to agencies of its choice.

Will this hurt street people, some of whom depend on direct handouts for survival?

"Sure. But it's a way of diverting money to programs for these people, instead of having it go for alcohol," Holmes said.

Yet Holmes knows full well that a percentage of chronic alcoholics and addicts on the street cannot be helped by programs. He knows they will live and die on the streets. So why would a compassionate man like Holmes advocate programs to dissuade direct giving? Because he has to appease a federal government that dangles money and demands the impossible task of ending homelessness in 10 years—something Holmes knows we cannot do.

If you're inclined to help people who fall through every crack, then give directly to people on the street. Just ignore these outrageous campaigns that tell us to always fund programs, but never to help an outstretched hand.

SIX

Giving Money to Panhandlers Does Not Help the Chronically Homeless

Derek Thompson

Derek Thompson is an associate editor at the *Atlantic*, where he writes about economics, business, and technology. In the following viewpoint Thompson argues that giving money directly to panhandlers is generally not very helpful to them. He cites a study showing that a majority of homeless people have problems with alcohol or other drugs, and claims that since homeless people usually have no way of saving money, they are likely to spend the money for immediate gratification (such as alcohol), rather than take care of their long-term needs. In Thompson's opinion, since people are more likely to give to those who seem needier, panhandlers are also motivated to lie about their situation or allow themselves to deteriorate instead of getting help. He believes it is a mistake to give money directly to a panhandler, and that instead longer-term solutions to the problem of homelessness need to be sought.

Giving money to the homeless is an economic crisis of the heart, a tug-of-war between the instinct to alleviate suffering and the knowledge that a donation might encourage, rather than relieve, the anguish of the poor.

We're all familiar with our mothers' reasons not to empty our pockets for beggars. "The best help is a shelter not a dollar," she's told us, and "They'll only use it on [something bad] anyway!"

The studies seem to back up mom, to a degree. One report from the Department of Housing and Urban Development found that six out of ten homeless respondents admitted problems with alcohol or drugs. Given the likelihood of self-reported bias, the actual number could be even higher. Studies on homeless income find that the typical "career panhandler" who dedicates his time overwhelmingly to begging can make between $600 and $1,500 a month. But since panhandlers often have no way to save their money, they're incentivized to spend most of their day's earnings quickly. This creates a tendency to spend on short-term relief, rather than long-term needs, which can feed this dependency on alcoholic relief.

The Case for Giving

What do economists say about the instinct to help the homeless? (For these purposes, I'm ignoring the altruism factor, the idea that if giving 50 cents makes us feel good then it's an inherently justifiable donation.) Some argue that giving cash to cash-needy people is the most efficient way to spend it. Indeed, the Congressional Budget Office has stated explicitly that the most efficient government stimulus targets the poorest Americans. And who's more indigent than a panhandler? What's more, if you donate to a charity, there are administrative costs and time-lags. If you put your money in the hands of a beggar, however, it's fast, easy, and guaranteed to be spent immediately.

But the fact that beggars are likely to spend their money quickly is also the problem. Food stamps are considered highly effective government spending, but they're earmarked for food. Unemployment benefits can go a long way, but recipients have

Homeless panhandlers have a tendency to spend their money on short-term relief through alcohol or other drugs rather than considering their long-term needs, the author contends.

to prove that they're looking for work. A dollar from your hand to a homeless person's carries no such strings attached.

But what would happen if we provided both money *and* strings? *Good* magazine found a British non-profit that identified 15 long-term homeless people ("rough sleepers," as they're known across the pond), asked what they needed to change their lives, and just bought it for them. Some asked for items as simple as shoes,

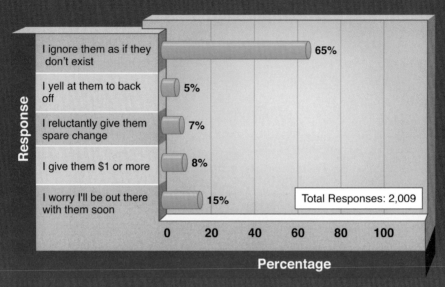

How People Deal with Panhandlers

Response

I ignore them as if they don't exist	65%
I yell at them to back off	5%
I reluctantly give them spare change	7%
I give them $1 or more	8%
I worry I'll be out there with them soon	15%

Total Responses: 2,009

0   20   40   60   80   100

Percentage

Taken from: "We've Gone Soft," *BostonHerald.com Blogs*, March 10, 2009. www.bostonherald.com/blogs/news/city _desk_wired/index.php/2009/03/10/1978/.

or cash to repay a loan. One asked for a camper van. Another wanted a TV to make his hostel more livable. All were accommodated with 3,000 pounds and a "broker" to help them manage their budget. Of the 13 who agreed to take part, 11 were off the street within a year, and several entered treatment for addiction.

The upshot: *The homeless often need something more than money. They need money and direction.* For most homeless people, direction means a job and a roof. A 1999 study from HUD polled homeless people about what they needed most: 42% said help finding a job; 38% said finding housing; 30% said paying rent or utilities; 13% said training or medical care.

What Should Be Done
Organizations can obviously do more for the needy than we can with the change in our back pocket. But does that mean we shouldn't give, *ever*?

The consistently entertaining economist Tyler Cowen worries that giving to beggars induces bad long-term incentives. If you travel to a poor city, for example, you'll find swarms of beggars by touristy locations. If the tourists become more generous, the local beggars don't get richer, they only multiply. Generous pedestrians attract more beggars. Cowen writes:

> The more you give to beggars, the harder beggars will try. This leads to what economists call "rent exhaustion," which again limits the net gain to beggars. . . . If you are going to give, pick the poor person who is expecting it least.

I'm certain that there are some cases where donations to an especially needy beggar are justified. But the ultimate danger in panhandling is that we don't give to every beggar. There's not enough change in our purses. We choose to donate money based on the level of perceived need. Beggars know this, so there is an incentive on their part to exaggerate their need, by either lying about their circumstances or letting their appearance visibly deteriorate rather than seek help.

If we drop change in a beggar's hand without donating to a charity, we're acting to relieve our guilt rather than underlying crisis of poverty. The same calculus applies to the beggar who relies on panhandling for a booze hit. In short, both sides fail each other by being lured into fleeting sense of relief rather than a lasting solution to the structural problem of homelessness.

SEVEN

More than Positive Thinking Is Needed to Deal with Homelessness

Anna Nussbaum Keating

> Anna Nussbaum Keating is a Catholic writer and teacher who lives in South Bend, Indiana. In the following viewpoint, Keating argues that there is a limit to how helpful positive thinking can be on the lives of the homeless. She says that she has seen many people who work with the homeless that have been strongly influenced by the "law of attraction"—the belief that people attract good or bad things into their lives through positive or negative thinking. According to Keating, some aspects of positive thinking can be helpful to the homeless, such as making collages of one's hopes and dreams. However, she suggests that suffering is much more complex than the simplistic interpretations of positive thinking would suggest. For example, a homeless student of hers who was first raped at the age of five clearly did not attract that violence into her life through negative thinking.

Shortly after graduating from the University of Notre Dame in 2006 with a degree in the program of liberal studies, I took a job doing adult education—teaching reading, writing, math and computers skills—at a homeless shelter, where the power of positive thinking was the staff drug of choice.

I knew social workers who stared at $100 bills before going to bed, hoping to attract "abundance" into their lives, rather than going into a more lucrative profession. And I once listened as our staff wellness expert handily dismissed the problem of evil in front of a class of homeless students using the same logic—that is, positive psychology's "law of attraction." This is the belief that positive energy attracts positive energy and negative energy attracts negative energy. So whatever happens to you, good or bad, you have attracted it by your thoughts. In short, if you are rich or famous, keep doing whatever it is you are doing. If you are poor, sick or suffering, you and only you are to blame. Think healthy prosperous thoughts . . . or else.

The Law of Attraction

Popularized by self-help literature, these ideas that whatever we desire we will have, that it is all in our heads, that we alone control our destinies and that "thoughts become things" have been around in various forms for a long time. But they have recently reemerged on a large scale with the enormous success of Rhonda

Cartoon © by Steve Greenberg. Reproduced by permission.

Byrne's book and movie by the same name, *The Secret*. The secret, of course, is the law of attraction. Oprah Winfrey swears by it; she has featured it multiple times on her television show and in her magazine, and millions of ordinary Americans are buying in. I have even seen *The Secret* advertised on the outside notice boards of South Bend [Indiana] area churches: "Unity Church of Peace knows The Secret, do you?"

So as the wellness expert and devotee of *The Secret* explained to my homeless students how they could vanquish their suffering and end their poverty with the power of positive energy, I wondered, a little shocked, what kind of energy the people of Iraq had been sending out into the ether, thus "attracting" such unrest. I did not allow myself to think about the woman in the front row, who, I knew from a writing assignment, had been raped for the first time at the age of 5. Certainly as a little child she had not attracted this violence. Its occurrence was something I could neither fathom nor wave away.

Of course, certain aspects of the positive-thinking curriculum seemed unremarkable: for instance, making "vision boards" with my homeless students (poster-board collages full of images symbolizing their hopes and dreams). This seemed fun and benign. After all, there is something to be said for visualizing one's own success. Still, giving students the necessary skills to go after the three-story house on the white board and suggesting that thinking about that house and getting it are magically interconnected by the power of positive thought are two very different things.

This troubling idea, that affliction is doled out as punishment for one's negative thoughts and that prosperity is a result of thinking positively, prompted me to reflect on my own understanding of suffering, informed at least in part by the writings of Blessed Julian of Norwich.

Meeting Suffering with Compassion

In *Revelations of Divine Love*, Julian offers no causal explanation for suffering. While she acknowledges human sinfulness, she also recognizes an unjust and fallen world in which all people suffer.

Rhonda Byrne's book The Secret *suggests that the homeless can end their suffering and rise out of poverty through the power of positive energy.*

In Julian's vision of the parable of the lord and the servant, a lord sends his servant on a journey. While traveling, the servant stumbles and falls in a dell. Trapped in the dell, injured and alone, the servant suffers greatly. Instead of being angry at the servant's clumsiness or sin, the lord mysteriously loves the servant more than ever. In this radical accounting, suffering is not simply negative, at least not in its entirety. Rather, it is sometimes the means through which humanity is drawn impossibly closer to God's self.

During my year at the homeless shelter, I was confronted daily with the realities of homelessness, rape, addiction, violence and mental illness. In that space, Julian's approach seemed not only more compassionate, but perhaps more helpful as well. Yes, our attitudes can and do positively improve our lives, but they do not explain suffering or success. All people suffer. We are not our own creations, tidy products of ideology. We are human beings, hopelessly interdependent, ugly and beautiful, both.

I was sitting in my office at the shelter doing paperwork one day when an especially cantankerous student came to my door. She did not want to do her worksheets. She did not want to work with a tutor. She did not want to sit and read. I gave her directions and showed her how to use a computer-typing program, but she came back every few minutes, needing help with the mouse.

It is not that difficult, I told her, looking down at her purple-stained lips and messy side ponytail. Pay attention, I said. She told me that it was hard for her to remember things ever since she was hit by a car while walking along the side of the highway collecting cans. Her body was thrown into a ditch, she told me. "I've had several brain surgeries," she added.

No, I cannot comprehend the suffering of these students. I can only trust that someone might be willing to venture into the dell with them, if only for a moment, neither of them helpless but both of them hoping in a God whose will is our peace.

EIGHT

Homeless People Need Compassion and Empathy

Gillie Easdon

> Gillie Easdon is a writer and publicist in Victoria, British Columbia, Canada. In the following viewpoint Easdon suggests that people who are homeless need to be met with compassion and empathy. She describes her experience of volunteering to work with the homeless and how it changed the way she felt about the issue and the people affected. Before her experience she says she avoided street homeless and would not make eye contact with them. Volunteering helped her to overcome her fear and to see the homeless as people who are not that different from her, but who have been caught in very difficult situations. As a result of her experience she reports gaining a deeper understanding of people who are homeless and their circumstances.

"Where is . . ." the man with the disheveled bedless-head struggled to ask the busy business-suited woman, who just recoiled and muttered an indeterminate "I dunno" into her Wildfire coffee and skittered away.

It was the morning of Project Connect during Homelessness Action Week, and I was off to London Drugs to procure extra nametags. I approached the man and asked, "Are you looking for the event?" His eyes lit upon mine, and he nodded. I pointed the way to St. John the Divine. "Will they have food for my cat?" he asked, his cheeks a strain of dusty red anguish and hope. "Yes, they have food for your cat," I replied. His smile is still lodged in my throat, along with my heart, and my "homeless people shouldn't have pets if they can't even afford to feed themselves" grumble fell away permanently.

Prior to volunteering for Project Connect, I did cross to the other side of the road when I saw a homeless person. I did not give change, but did buy the newspaper some of them sell. I did not make eye contact as a general rule. I housed and nurtured fear, disgust and antipathy, along with an ignorance of the plight of homeless people, for which I was ashamed. At least I recognized that.

As a Cormorant Street resident who foolishly prides herself on being somewhat educated, worldly and compassionate (i.e.: I choose one charity a year to donate to and I volunteer—yay me), I confess all of the above, not seeking validation or vindication. I felt frustrated and helpless to do anything but bitch about the "homeless problem," which left a bad taste in my mouth because, again, I simply did not know what I was talking about.

Volunteering to Help the Homeless

So when an e-mail went around that Jody Patterson and the Greater Victoria Coalition to End Homelessness were putting on an event for—not about—homeless people, I immediately signed up to volunteer. Because I needed to address my own misconceptions and put myself in a situation to be with the people I avoid; to humanize those whose humanity I, in my own precious mind-world, had denied. Who am I, really, to judge? (But, of course, I do.)

Over the next couple of days, I found myself considering the homeless I saw on my dogwalk beat. I wondered if I would see them at Project Connect and if we would talk. I bit my nails; part of me really wanted to bail.

I met with Jody and a couple other volunteers at the Red Dragon cafe. Jody explained that the point of the event was to

Violence in the Lives of Homeless Children

83% of homeless children have been exposed to at least one serious violent event by the age of twelve.

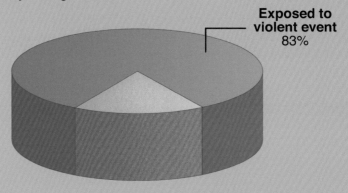

Exposed to
violent event
83%

Taken from: "Children," The National Center on Family Homelessness, 2010. www.familyhomelessness.org/children.php?p=ts/.

dialogue with homeless people and learn what they need, what they want. The Coalition to End Homelessness had never actually done this, which baffled me, but did make me feel a little less like an idiot. Project Connect sought to feed approximately 500 homeless, and there would also be services available, such as a nurse, vet, acupuncturist, welfare, housing and ID information, haircuts and Cool Aid, to name a few.

The day before the event, about 20 volunteers gathered at St. John the Divine to divide and package the onslaught of donations into 500 survival packs. Each kit would contain, at the very least, shampoo, soap, hand sanitizer, gloves, toothpaste, brush and assorted extras that could be a toque or a scarf, shaving gel, fruit leather, etc. Three tampons each for women. (Homeless with your period; I never thought of that.) I came across a donated bag of lipsticks. "What do they need this for?" was my silent immediate reaction, for which I felt embarrassed.

On the day of the event, I met Jeff and Gena (not their real names). One of our jobs as volunteers was to survey the guests; Jeff and Gena were the first survey I did. They had saved up money

These homeless men live in Vancouver, British Columbia, Canada. The Canadian Project Connect program strives to meet the problems of the homeless with compassion and empathy.

to come out from Ontario; Jeff was a tradesman, but he had hurt his back badly; they were both needle-users and Gena was also mentally unwell; they only had $500 a month to live on. Jeff said "needle-user" with the same fact-stating tone as someone shares their birthday or hair colour. But honestly, they were kind folks who were stuck and just thankful to attend Project Connect.

A Different Perspective

In short, the day was full of nice, helpful people. Polite people. And yes, some were drunk and some were strung out and some did not "look homeless" at all. There were two small incidents, but no calamities; approach people with respect and friendliness and they respond in kind—that's what I remembered at Project Connect (and kindergarten). After eight hours on-site, the event ended and we packed up. Two out of the three homeless people I was keeping an eye out for from my dogwalk beat didn't show up.

Afterwards, I walked home with an unprecedented sense of calm. I nodded to the woman with the shopping cart and did not look away. It was not a conscious choice; it just happened and I noticed. Since Project Connect, my downtown—any home—feels more full. There are not pockets that I don't look at now.

I still hear the wailing in the middle of the night, I don't want to step on needles and I don't think that homeless people should be able to just sleep all over the city. I don't think Pandora Street and the Victoria Conservatory of Music and Blair Mart should have to bear the brunt of the city's non-action. And it still boggles my mind that some able homeless people think they should be bankrolled and not have to pitch in like the rest of us. But I don't glare at people who are obviously already down. I don't know their stories (plural), but if there are not enough beds, where are people supposed to sleep? I knew I had been ignorant, but I hadn't really processed that I was part of the problem.

Anger permeated my body for a few days following Project Connect. I was angry at the smug "We know what it's like" response I got from a couple of people at a cafe, angry at those whose reactions to my participating in the event was an equally smug, "Oh, well done. That was good of you"—but it's only anger at my own previous smugness projected on those around me.

It wouldn't really be all that hard for many of us to end up on the street, barring our friends, bank account, family support, physical and mental health. What would have to happen for you to be homeless? Just try it in your head. Take away all that stuff that makes you you. No wonder people on the street scare so many of us.

As George Bernard Shaw said, "The worst sin towards our fellow creatures is not to hate them, but to be indifferent to them; that's the essence of inhumanity."

NINE

Blind Compassion Does Not Help the Homeless

Jayne Sorrels

Jayne Sorrels is executive director of an interfaith home-less shelter in Boise, Idaho, and director/founder of the Viriditas Center, an ecumenical center for Contemplative Christianity committed to supporting individuals pursuing an integrated path of contemplation and engaged com-passion. In the following viewpoint Sorrels argues that to simply give people what they want—as opposed to what they really need—is to act from blind, or "idiot," com-passion. She believes that sometimes people need to be confronted and their bad behavior disallowed for their own sake or that of others. She describes an experience she had as a homeless-shelter manager, in which she had to call the police to evict a homeless couple on a very cold night because their bad behavior was disrupting the entire shelter. Reflecting on that experience deepened her understanding of the nature of true compassion.

I have been working to understand compassion and learn how to apply it in my work and life for the past several years. Recently, however, I've been looking at compassion from a different perspec-tive. When does compassion not really look like compassion—or how we have been led to believe compassion *should* look? When is it more compassionate to be fierce? To say no? To hold another accountable for their actions? And how can we use true compassion to effectively serve another?

As a homeless shelter manager, I am called to make decisions every day that test my understanding of genuine compassion. It's been a learning experience over these past two years. The first time I needed to hold someone truly accountable for their behavior, it tore me apart. I needed to call the police on a couple who was causing such chaos in the shelter that they were taking the house down. Everyone wanted them out and we were in a one-room warehouse at the time. It was COLD outside—like really cold! And, I liked them. I, of course, worked with them every which way I could think of to calm them down so everyone could sleep. When nothing worked and they wouldn't leave on their own accord, I called the police to escort them out. As they left, the woman looked at me and said "I curse you. Our lives are in your hands." Geez! After they left, I went in the back alley and cried. When I got home that night, I did prayer ceremonies for them both. That was two years ago. I think it took them a few months to get over it and since then our paths have crossed frequently through the street outreach work I do and all is quite well between us.

Giving People What They Want Instead of What They Need

Idiot (or blind) compassion is a term that was introduced by Chogyam Trungpa Rinpoche and refers to the tendency of spiritual practitioners to give people what they *want* as opposed to what they *need*, all in the name of being nice and compassionate. In an effort to maintain harmony, one takes the limited view of what the ego wants versus what the soul actually needs to grow.

> Idiot compassion is the highly conceptualized idea that you want to do good to somebody. At this point, good is purely related with pleasure. Idiot compassion also stems from not having enough courage to say no.
>
> —Chogyam Trungpa

"Sidestep the real issue $5." Cartoon by Mike Baldwin. www.CartoonStock.com © Mike Baldwin. Reproduction rights obtainable from www.CartoonStock.com.

Robert Augustus Masters defines blind compassion as "neurotically tolerant, confrontation-phobic, indiscriminating caring."

Blind compassion is commonly centered by the belief that everyone is doing the best they can. Not surprisingly, blind compassion cuts everyone—*everyone*—far too much slack, making an ever-so-gentle fuss about not making a fuss regarding behavioral lapses it is taking pains to so kindly address. . . .

Very rarely does blind compassion show any anger, for it's scared to upset anyone. This is reinforced by its negative conceptualizing of anger, especially in its more fiery expression, as something less than spiritual, something equated with ill will, hostility, and aggression, something that should not be there if we are being truly loving. Blind compassion has the mistaken notion that compassion has to be gentle.

Blind compassion has no voice, other than that of making nice and making excuses; its articulation is relentlessly soft and pleasant, brightly buttoned-up. No guts. Being a harmony junkie, blind compassion will do just about anything to keep the peace, so long as it doesn't have to show its teeth in anything other than I-wouldn't-harm-a-fly smiles. . . .

When those who espouse blind compassion encounter offensive behavior from others, they usually take pains to not only be nonjudgmental (or at least not to say or do anything that could be construed as judgmental), but also to examine whatever such behavior may be triggering in them, while bringing no significant heat to those who are actually behaving offensively. That is, if what you are doing is upsetting me, my job (as a graduate of Blind Compassion 101) is not to focus to any significant degree on your behavior, but rather to find out what my being bothered says about me, while perhaps also acknowledging and appreciating the opportunity you are giving me to examine myself.

This is not only a misguided reading of the art of allowing all things to serve our awakening, but also a far-from-compassionate response to our offending others, for we, in not being on the side of doing what we can to bring them face to face with the consequences of their actions, are on the side of depriving them of something they may sorely need. And in letting them off the hook, we are doing the same for ourselves.

A caseworker advises a homeless person. Blind compassion for the homeless has come under fire for giving the homeless what they want—but not what they need.

Love Can Be Fierce

Masters suggests that to effectively deal with blind compassion that we get familiar with it.

> Don't get pulled into its embrace. See it, name it, don't blame it. Meet it and its underlying fear with genuine compassion, compassion that's willing to be fiery, fierce, unsmiling, compassion that is loving enough not to give a damn about being nice. As blind compassion sheds its masks, and opens its eyes to its own pain, its own anger and hurt and frustration and moral outrage, thereby letting in a love previously not accessible, it loses its blind nature, and simply

becomes compassion, with an especially keen eye for those who are still under the spell of blind compassion.

One of the greatest leaps in my understanding of genuine compassion is that if you are truly centered in love and are coming from the place of compassion, then if it is called for to be fierce, to hold others accountable for their actions, or to make hard decisions—that they will receive this well. They may be angry in the moment, but it will pass. I believe that when you come from the place of blind compassion, you are (in a way) demeaning the other person—holding them in a vision that is less than what they are capable of . . . asking too little.

In working with the practice of genuine compassion, a number of questions arise for me:

- Can I handle people getting mad at me because I'm not playing to their ego-centered desires—what they *want* versus what they *need*?
- Can I get over potential disapproval or judgment when others view me as unkind, unsympathetic, or even cold?
- Do I have enough awareness of my own shadow tendencies to have clarity on what is a genuine compassionate response and what's not?
- How can I remain centered in the space of absolute compassion and love while still holding others responsible for their actions, choices, etc.?
- How comfortable am I in the presence of another's pain and suffering?
- How can I effectively navigate around my aversion to conflict?
- How can I get over the idea that I am causing another harm (or potentially causing harm) when I hold them accountable for their choices? How can I shift my thinking from the short-term view to an eternal perspective?

TEN

Some Homeless People Are Taking Advantage of Support Systems

Becky Blanton

> Becky Blanton has twenty-two years of experience as a journalist and photojournalist. She spoke at the Technology, Entertainment, Design conference, TEDGlobal 2009, in Oxford, England, about being one of the "working homeless" and about her time living in a van for a year in Denver, Colorado. In the following viewpoint Blanton argues that some homeless people could easily get out of homelessness but choose to remain stuck in their situation and to falsely define themselves as victims. She distinguishes such people from those who genuinely need help because they are incapable of overcoming their situations by themselves, due to disability or some other adverse circumstance. According to Blanton, too many resources are wasted on people who could get off the street if they wanted to, instead of going toward people who can really use the help and who are motivated to improve their situations.

One of the most curious things I've learned about the word "homeless" is that there's not one accepted definition. A reporter who wanted to do a story on me a while back was confused and annoyed because the photos I had of me "being homeless" weren't depressing enough.

"Who smiles when they're homeless?" she asked.

Well, lots of people actually. It's not like being homeless makes you a 24/7 poster child for Prozac [the drug often prescribed to treat depression]. It sucks, but for many of us, it has its good moments—being with friends, scoring a great meal or being handed $20 you weren't expecting, wearing new clothes or socks, getting a job, savoring a balmy summer evening with a safe place to sleep. You can have good days when you're homeless. Really. You aren't betraying anyone or living a lie if you laugh while living on the streets or in your car. You might be accused of not truly being homeless if you aren't in abject misery around the clock, but who cares?

When I was on the streets of Denver the homeless I met there often told me I wasn't homeless because I "had hope." Where I lived (a van) had nothing to do with my homeless designation. My attitude did. They saw that as down and depressed as I was, I wasn't totally resigned to continuing to live as I was.

There are still people who tell me that because I lived in a van I wasn't "really" homeless. To a large segment of our population, apparently "being homeless" involves being unemployed and addicted, covered in your own feces, crawling with lice, reeking of body odor and begging for cigarettes on the street. A box or viaduct or culvert is acceptable shelter if you want to meet the "truly homeless" standard, but a van, car or tent in a National Park isn't. You aren't or haven't been "really homeless" until you've lost everything, everybody and all connection to society. If, at any time you have any kind of resource or edge—you're not really homeless. I call bullpuckey on that.

So I've recently decided there are two kinds of homeless people. There are victims, and there are the rest of us. Victims have neither options nor hope; the homeless have no house.

There are people who for mental health reasons, age, disability and some other circumstances will always be homeless victims no matter how much they don't want to be. They no more have the ability, resources or options to get off the street than I have to play basketball in the NBA. They truly have no options unless they find an agency or organization that is willing and able to do for them what they cannot do for themselves. They are victims—unfortunate people who suffer adversity through no fault of their own.

Choosing to Be a Victim

Then there are other kinds of "victims." These are the people who revel in their homelessness, in being at rock bottom—because it is the ultimate badge of victimhood. No van, no family, no friends, no hope. They take pride in being homeless and have no desire to get off the streets even though they *may* have the ability to do so. They enjoy being a victim for a variety of reasons, from attention-seeking to an ignorance that there's a better way. Anyone who threatens their reality, or their ability to remain a victim, or who

Homeless people line up for food distribution in Barstow, California. Many of the homeless are in genuine need, but others revel in their homelessness and seek out organizations that allow them to abuse the system.

suggests they might really be able to change their status as a victim, is seen as a threat or an uncaring, insensitive bastard.

Worse, these people find organizations that enable them in their victim status—organizations that continue to warehouse them and allow them to abuse the system in order to retain funding and jobs for the organization. There are thousands of organizations content to let marginal victims be victims. I'm not alone in seeing this.

Remember, I am *not* blaming people who have been legitimately victimized. I'm just saying there are people who are truly victims and there are those who are truly not. Anyone who has ever worked in or stayed in a shelter or been on the streets knows the difference.

Labeling someone "not really homeless" is one way some people preserve their victim status and divert attention and resources to themselves. By insisting that those who are working hard to get off of the street "aren't really homeless," they preserve their status as the pitiful and hopeless—whether they are or not.

So, what makes someone *truly* homeless? And does it matter? I spoke with Ed Brenegar a few months ago about this. Ed is a life coach, a business leader and a pastor. He has worked with the homeless for decades and has seen and had a hand in some miraculous recoveries, such as addicts and alcoholics no one else would work with. He's helped them get off the streets and into productive, happy lives. He was able to because they wanted off the streets. They fit the typical "homeless" model of people truly at the bottom of life's barrel yet they escaped the streets. Why? Hope. Attitude. Desire.

Gaming the System

Ed struggles with this dichotomy as well. We talked at length about two men he met who were both working, both making enough at day jobs to afford food and a campground and bus fare, but not enough to save for a car. They utilized homeless services and considered themselves homeless but weren't quite "homeless enough" to get the little bit of help they needed to move beyond

" *Talk about a stressful day . . THREE people offered me jobs !* "

"Talk about a Stressful day . . . THREE people offered me jobs!" Cartoon by Roy Delgado/www .CartoonStock.com. © Roy Delgado. Reproduction rights obtainable from www.CartoonStock.com

their situation. They weren't victims, so they didn't qualify for help as homeless.

Ed and I are both frustrated with a system for the homeless that focuses so many resources and so much energy on those victims who could get off the streets but don't want to, while ignoring those who, given a chance, some life skills and some breaks, could easily get off the streets and back on track. We struggled to define what it was that keeps so many homeless programs and shelters from being effective.

I met many homeless victims in Denver. They bragged about gaming and working the system, about getting free food, free rent and free services so they could continue to live free without work- ing. Some were addicts and alcoholics, others were young, healthy and capable of working and admitted it. They just didn't want to work and told me society "owed" them. Sorry guys—it's true. Not everyone on the streets is a hard luck story waiting for a happy ending—which is why the current economic situation has upset the victim cart.

There are more and more homeless people and families because of economic or temporary life situations. They don't want to be victims and resent the implication that they are. They don't want to linger in the homeless holding pattern. They want out. They want options. They're not about to give up any chance to feel empowered and in control. They know that feeling empowered is what they need to get off of the streets. They're demanding real help—life skills classes, job coaching, transitional housing, affordable housing. They want to read about how others beat the street and made it back into a job or house. They're house-less, but not hope-less.

There are definitely two camps. And as the economy worsens, the differences will become more obvious. I for one hope that in time the word homeless will stop being synonymous with the word victim.

ELEVEN

Promoting Access to Technology Can Help the Homeless

Joel John Roberts

Joel John Roberts is the chief executive officer of the nonprofit organization People Assisting the Homeless (PATH) and the author of *How to Increase Homelessness*. He publishes www.PovertyInsights.org, a national online journal for poverty and homelessness. In the following viewpoint Roberts argues that technology such as the Apple iPad could be used to help the homeless in a wide variety of ways, such as locating emergency and support services, accessing job listings, writing resumes, and joining online communities for a sense of belonging. He says it may seem crazy to give equipment worth $500 to homeless people, but cites a study in 2009 that found that the cost for public benefits, emergency rooms, and law enforcement for a homeless person in Los Angeles amounted to $2,897 per month. Roberts gives examples of websites that come close to the kind of resources he has in mind.

It has only been one year, but it feels like 10. Not how fast time goes by while raising children. Not the rapid pace from one birthday to another. I am referring to the length of time this world has experienced integrating a thin piece of electronic glass and metal into our every day lives.

One year since Apple introduced the iPad.

Remember those long lines outside Apple Stores? Remember those congratulatory high fives by young employees sporting Apple T-shirts when you walked out of the door with your brand new iPad? You felt like you just opened a Willy Wonka chocolate bar and found the golden ticket.

This appliance that Apple defines as magical has revolutionized how society operates. Universities issue textbooks via iPad rather than the local bookstore. Church-goers read the Bible through a plate of glass rather than between leather binding. Businessmen are tapping on glass while jetting from one city to another instead of keyboards. Restaurants issue iPads rather than printed menus. You would have to be a hermit to not see a person hugging his iPad. Literally.

People are starting to read books more. Watch the news. Kids want to learn. People want to buy. The world is talking to each other via Facebook and Twitter.

One year. My, how time flies when there is magic in the air.

"THANK YOU, SIR. AND WOULD YOU LIKE TO BE ADDED TO MY DATABASE?"

Cartoon © by Harley Schwadron. Reproduced by permission.

How iPads Could Help the Homeless

I wonder if this magic could cross sectors? Reading, learning, buying, and talking is great. But what about helping someone find permanent housing? And I don't mean Zillow.com or Redfin.com [sites that list homes for sale and connect people to real estate agents]. Could this appliance magically help a homeless person find a home or pad of his own? Now, that would truly redefine the definition of iPad. Think: My pad. My home.

But if you are on the extreme bottom of the economic ladder in this country, a $500 electronic device is just out of reach. Besides, if the homeless agencies I direct started passing out expensive iPads, most people would think we are crazy.

"Homeless people will just sell them for drugs!" I am sure jaded housed people would say. But in 2009, the Economic Roundtable studied nearly 10,000 homeless persons in Los Angeles County and discovered that the public cost (emergency rooms, public benefits, law enforcement) for these people was $2,897 per month.

$500 doesn't sound so high any more. So how could an iPad help a homeless person find permanent housing?

For many people who encounter homeless persons on a daily basis, a handheld device that lists where all the services and housing for homeless people are located would really be magical. While designing a plan to address homelessness in a region of Los Angeles County, we encountered numerous law enforcement agency leaders who told us, "We just don't know where to send homeless people for help."

An iPad app that provided a list of life-changing housing resources could help the local librarian, nurse, church secretary, police officer and crossing guard when they encounter a homeless person seeking help. Some computer-based websites teeter toward this solution, including 211LA.org, socialserve.com and idealistics.org.

Online Community Support

An iPad filled with employment resources could change people's lives. We all know housing and employment provides dignity for

Although iPad technology can provide the homeless with access to services, online support, and housing, finding ways for the homeless to access the technology is difficult.

a person. An appliance that helps you write a resume, peruse job listings, and actually allows you to email letters and resumes to potential employers could transform the definition of employment training.

For many people living on the streets, homelessness means isolation. We all need a community of supporters, whether we are house-less or housed. Homeless advocate, Mark Horvath, created a very special online community for homeless folks via WeAreVisible.com. Wouldn't it be magical if truly supportive communities could be built on the streets with electronic devices that promote such online communities?

Apple says that the iPad is magical because it is a computer that can be held and touched. This is what those of us on the frontlines of homelessness value. We want to embrace people's lives so that they feel dignified, so that they have the will to overcome the barriers of the streets.

We want to touch people's lives with the gift of housing. A home provides security, dignity, protection, community, identity, and love.

A pad, a home is truly magical.

TWELVE

Homelessness Has a Serious Impact on Families and Children

National Coalition for the Homeless

The National Coalition for the Homeless (NCH) is a national network of people who are currently experiencing or who have experienced homelessness, activists and advocates, community-based and faith-based service providers, and others committed to the goal of ending homelessness. In the following viewpoint, the author argues that many families and children are experiencing homelessness, contrary to the popular belief that only single people are affected. The coalition notes recent trends of increased homelessness among families and children, citing a number of relevant statistics. According to the author, budget cutbacks and changes in various public programs, as well as the declining economy and other circumstances, have had an adverse impact on families, putting many more at risk of homelessness. The coalition contends that homelessness has many negative effects on families and children, such as more mental health issues and delayed development of children, increased risk of suicide, and family breakups.

There is a common misconception that homelessness is an issue that only pertains to single men and women, but in reality thousands of families a year will experience homelessness. In fact, 41% of the homeless population is comprised of families. Homelessness is a devastating experience for families. It disrupts virtually every aspect of family life, damaging the physical and emotional health of family members, interfering with children's education and development, and frequently resulting in the separation of family members. The problem of family homelessness is not solely restricted to urban areas; rural and suburban communities are increasingly plagued by the problem. President [Barack] Obama recently [February 2009] addressed this vital issue when he stated, "It is not acceptable for children and families to be without a roof over their heads in a country as wealthy as ours." The issue has become even more pressing recently in light of the severe economic downturn [as of December 2007] and the ensuing loss of jobs. Recent economic turmoil will assuredly lead to more families becoming homeless, testing already strained resources for homeless families. The numbers . . . used in this report are mostly from before the economic downturn, due to the time and manpower it takes to assemble statistics concerning homelessness. With this in mind the statistics mentioned in this report most likely understate the severity of the issue. The looming and disastrous possibility of increased family homelessness makes understanding the issue immensely pertinent. The dimensions, causes, and consequences of family homelessness are discussed below. . . .

Dimensions of Homelessness

One of the fastest growing segments of the homeless population are families with children. In 2007, 23% of all homeless people were members of families with children. Recent evidence confirms that homelessness among families is increasing. The rate of requests for emergency assistance by families rose faster than the rate for any other group between 2006 and 2007. In some cities, it rose by as much as 15%. 71% of cities surveyed reported an increase in the number of families with children

A homeless family moves into a shelter. Homelessness can have a devastating effect on children, as well as damaging a family's entire dynamic.

seeking emergency assistance. Every single one of the 23 cities surveyed expected an increase in the number of families with children seeking assistance in 2008. Additionally, a recent report by the Department of Housing and Urban Development (HUD) reported that the number of people in families that were homeless rose by 9 percent from Oct. 1, 2007, to Sept. 30, 2008. This is a disconcerting statistic in light of the previously mentioned fact that the country's economic troubles were just beginning to accelerate as of September 2008. Furthermore, there is another reason to believe the numbers might actually be higher; homeless families often double up with other families. This causes them to be exempt from the federal definition of chronic homelessness, which states that a chronically homeless person is one who is on the streets or in a shelter. Therefore, many homeless families are not counted and prevented from receiving assistance.

It is clear that the problem of family homelessness is accelerating, but meanwhile services to accommodate the increasing numbers are lagging behind. While the average number of emergency shelter beds for homeless families with children increased by 8% in 2005, an average of 32% of requests for shelter by homeless families were denied in 2005 due to lack of resources.

In addition to the lack of resources to combat the problem the most pressing issue involved with family homelessness is the plight of the children involved. Estimates of the number of homeless children range from 800,000 to 1.2 million, and recent [2009] estimates state that 1 in 50 children in the United States are homeless. What's more, at least half of homeless children are under the age of 5.

Causes of Homelessness

Poverty and the lack of affordable housing are the principal causes of family homelessness. While the number of poor people decreased every year between 1993 and 2000, in recent years the number and percentage of poor people has increased. The percentage of poor people has risen from 11.3% of the population in 2000 to 12.1 % in 2002, and by 2004 the number of poor people grew by 4.3 million from 2000. Today, 35.2% of persons living in poverty are children; in fact, the 2004 poverty rate of 17.8% for children under 18 years old is significantly higher than the poverty rate for any other age group.

Declining wages and changes in welfare programs account for increasing poverty among families. Declining wages have put housing out of reach for many families: in every state, metropolitan area, county, and town, more than the minimum wage is required to afford a one- or two-bedroom apartment at Fair Market Rent. In fact, the median wage needed to afford a two-bedroom apartment is more than twice the minimum wage. Until its repeal in August 1996, the largest cash assistance program for poor families with children was the Aid to Families with Dependent Children

(AFDC) program. Between 1970 and 1994, the typical state's AFDC benefits for a family of three fell 47%, after adjusting for inflation. The Personal Responsibility and Work Opportunity Reconciliation Act of 1996 (the federal welfare reform law) repealed the AFDC program and replaced it with a block grant program called Temporary Assistance to Needy Families (TANF). Current TANF benefits and Food Stamps combined are below the poverty level in every state; in fact, the median TANF benefit for a family of three is approximately one-third of the poverty level. In addition, as the percentage and number of poor people has increased in recent years, the number of people receiving TANF has decreased. Between 2000 and 2003 the number of poor children rose 11%, and during this same period, the number of people receiving TANF fell by nine percent. Thus, contrary to popular opinion, welfare does not provide relief from poverty.

Welfare caseloads have dropped sharply since the passage and implementation of welfare reform legislation. However, declining welfare rolls simply mean that fewer people are receiving benefits—not that they are employed or doing better financially. Early findings suggest that although more families are moving from welfare to work, many of them are faring poorly due to low wages and inadequate work supports. Only a small fraction of welfare recipients' new jobs pay above-poverty wages; most of the new jobs pay far below the poverty line. Moreover, extreme poverty is growing more common for children, especially those in female-headed and working families. This increase can be traced directly to the declining number of children lifted above one-half of the poverty line by government cash assistance for the poor.

A Chronic Housing Shortage

As a result of loss of benefits, low wages, and unstable employment, many families leaving welfare struggle to get medical care, food, and housing. . . . Housing is rarely affordable for families leaving welfare for low wages, yet subsidized housing is so limited that fewer than one in four TANF families nationwide lives in public housing or receives a housing voucher to help them rent a

Main Causes of Family Homelessness

Mayors from twenty-five big cities reported on the main causes of family homelessness.

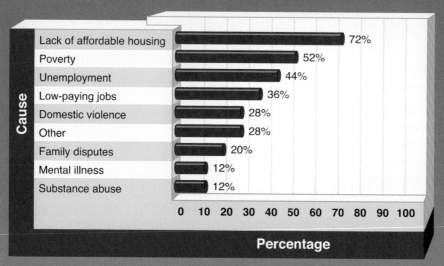

Source: "Exhibit 2.6. Causes of Family Homelessness," in *Hunger and Homelessness Survey: A Status Report on Hunger and Homelessness in America's Cities, A 25-City Survey*, U.S. Conference of Mayors, December 2008, http://www.usmayors.org/pressreleases/documents/hungerhomelessnessreport_121208.pdf.

Taken from: Melissa J. Doak, *Social Welfare: Fighting Poverty and Homelessness*, Farmington Hills, MI: Gale, 2010.

private unit. For most families leaving the rolls, housing subsidies are not an option. In some communities, former welfare families appear to be experiencing homelessness in increasing numbers.

A shortage of housing options for poor families is a problem that exists no matter the economic conditions. When the economy was strong, rental rates soared as a result of the housing bubble, making it difficult for poorer families to find affordable rental housing. After the 1980s, income growth has never kept pace with rents, and since 2000, the incomes of low-income households has declined as rents continue to rise. Once the housing bubble burst and the economy fell on hard times the problem did not subsist. Poorer families had to contend with two large issues, an increase in competition for rental properties, which sustained high prices and the loss of income that comes with layoffs and job losses. This situation is another factor underlying the growth in family homelessness. In 2004 the average wait for Section 8 Vouchers [a federal program that helps very low income families to afford housing in the private market] was 35 months. Excessive waiting lists for public housing mean that families must remain in shelters or inadequate housing arrangements longer. Consequently, there is less shelter space available for other homeless families, who must find shelter elsewhere or live on the streets.

Domestic violence also contributes to homelessness among families. When a woman leaves an abusive relationship, she often has nowhere to go. This is particularly true of women with few resources. Lack of affordable housing and long waiting lists for assisted housing mean that many women are forced to choose between abuse and the streets. In a study of 777 homeless parents (the majority of whom were mothers) in ten U.S. cities, 22% said they had left their last place of residence because of domestic violence. In addition, 50% of the cities surveyed by the U.S. Conference of Mayors identified domestic violence as a primary cause of homelessness. Nationally, approximately half of all women and children experiencing homelessness are fleeing domestic violence.

The situation is dire; these families are facing a tough job market, a shortage of affordable housing, restricted access to healthcare, and maybe domestic violence. These families are only a lost job, a paycheck, an illness, or an act of domestic violence away from becoming homeless.

Consequences of Family Homelessness

Homelessness severely impacts the health and well being of all family members. Children without a home are in fair or poor health twice as often as other children, and have higher rates of asthma, ear infections, stomach problems, and speech problems. Homeless children also experience more mental health problems, such as anxiety, depression, and withdrawal. They are twice as likely to experience hunger, and four times as likely to have delayed development. These illnesses have potentially devastating consequences if not treated early.

Deep poverty and housing instability are especially harmful during the earliest years of childhood; alarmingly, it is estimated that almost half of children in shelter are under the age of five. School-age homeless children face barriers to enrolling and attending school, including transportation problems, residency requirements, inability to obtain previous school records, and lack of clothing and school supplies.

Parents also suffer the ill effects of homelessness and poverty. One study of homeless and low-income housed families found that both groups experienced higher rates of depressive disorders than the overall female population, and that one-third of homeless mothers (compared to one-fourth of poor housed mothers) had made at least one suicide attempt. In both groups, over one-third of the sample had a chronic health condition.

Homelessness frequently breaks up families. Families may be separated as a result of shelter policies which deny access to older boys or fathers. Separations may also be caused by placement of children into foster care when their parents become homeless. In addition, parents may leave their children with relatives and friends in order to save them from the ordeal of homelessness or to permit them to continue attending their regular school. The break-up of families is a well-documented phenomenon: in 56% of the 27 cities surveyed in 2004, homeless families had to break up in order to enter emergency shelters.

Policy Issues

Policies to end homelessness must include jobs that pay livable wages. In order to work, families with children need access to quality childcare that they can afford, and adequate transportation. Education and training are also essential elements in preparing parents for better paying jobs to support their families.

But jobs, childcare, and transportation are not enough. Without affordable, decent housing people cannot keep their jobs and they cannot remain healthy. A recent [1998] longitudinal study of poor and homeless families in New York City found that regardless of social disorders, 80% of formerly homeless families who received subsidized housing stayed stably housed, i.e. lived in their own residence for the previous 12 months. In contrast, only 18% of the families who did not receive subsidized housing were stable at the end of the study. As this study and others demonstrate, affordable housing is a key component to resolving family homelessness. Preventing poverty and homelessness also requires access to affordable health care, so that illness and accidents no longer threaten to throw individuals and families into the streets.

HUD recently announced that $1.2 billion of stimulus money from The American Recovery and Reinvestment Act of 2009 has been allotted to combat homelessness. Hopefully, a proportional amount of this money will be used to combat the issues that specifically lead to the increasingly problematic situation of family homelessness in the United States.

Only concerted efforts to meet all of these needs will end the tragedy of homelessness for America's families and children.

THIRTEEN

Lesbian, Gay, Bisexual, and Transgender Homeless Youth Face Special Challenges

Anthony Glassman

Anthony Glassman is a staff reporter at *Gay People's Chronicle*, a newspaper in Ohio serving the lesbian, gay, bisexual, and transgender (LGBT) community. In the following viewpoint Glassman argues that LGBT youth are much more likely to be homeless than the general population. He provides quotes and statistics from a 2007 report jointly conducted by the National Gay and Lesbian Task Force and the National Coalition for the Homeless that details the problems faced by LGBT homeless youth, noting, for example, that youth are often kicked out of their homes when they reveal, or are discovered to have, unconventional sexual or gender orientations. According to Glassman, homeless LGBT youth are at increased risk of sexual victimization, harassment, and discrimination, including from homeless support organizations. He also says that LGBT youth, due to the discrimination and stigmatization they face, are more likely to have chemical dependency or mental health issues.

Two weeks after the Cleveland LGBT [lesbian, gay, bisexual, and transgender] Center began intensive outreach to homeless youth [in 2007], the National Gay and Lesbian Task Force [NGLTF] and the National Coalition for the Homeless [NCH] have released a report on the epidemic of homelessness among LGBT youth.

The most immediate information coming from the report, *An Epidemic of Homelessness*, is that 20 to 40 percent of homeless youth nationally identify themselves as LGBT, at least two to four times the average of the general population.

"This report underscores what we've known for a long time," said Matt Foreman, executive director of the NGLTF, "there is an epidemic of homelessness among LGBT youth and the national response to it has been disgraceful."

"There are a multitude of reasons why these young people become homeless, but ultimately family conflict is the ultimate reason," said Nicholas Ray, the author of the report. "The crisis begins with family conflict and institutionalized homophobia."

Higher Rates of Chemical Dependency and Mental Health Issues

The organizations presented a press conference announcing the release of the report on January 30 [2007]. Among the speakers was Angelika Torres, a transgendered Latina 20-year-old who was kicked out of her home because she refused to present herself as male.

Also speaking was Dilo Cintrón, 25, who was homeless for five years after being shuttled from one relative to another between the Virgin Islands and New York City.

When he was outed by a teacher, his parents sent him to live with an uncle in New York, without telling him that his nephew was gay.

Among the problems facing LGBT homeless youth are an increase in mental health issues, including depression, loneliness, psychosomatic illness, withdrawal and delinquency.

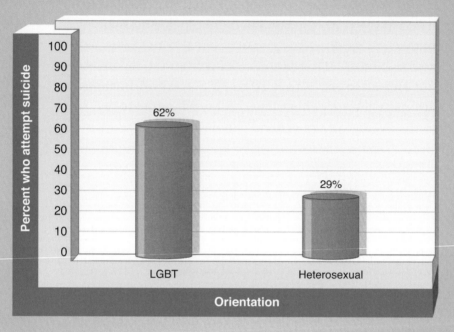

Suicide Attempts Among Heterosexual Homeless Youth and LGBT (Lesbian, Gay, Bisexual, Transgender) Homeless Youth

Taken from: "National Recommended Best Practices for Serving LGBT Homeless Youth," National Alliance to End Homelessness, April 10, 2009. www.endhomelessness.org/content/general/detail/2239.

"According to the U.S. Department of Health and Human Services, the fact that LGBT youth live in 'a society that discriminates against and stigmatizes homosexuals' makes them more vulnerable to mental health issues than heterosexual youth," the report's executive summary states. "This vulnerability is only magnified for LGBT youth who are homeless."

One of the consequences of those mental health issues is increased drug use.

"For example, in Minnesota, five separate statewide studies found that between 10 and 20 percent of homeless youth self-identify as chemically dependent. These risks are exacerbated for homeless youth identifying as lesbian, gay or bisexual," the report states.

Homeless sexual minority youth also face victimization both from society at large and, often, from the very organizations that are supposed to be helping them.

A Canadian study noted that LGBT homeless youth were three times more likely to engage in "survival sex," exchanging it for food, shelter, clothing, money, or drugs than their heterosexual, non-transgendered counterparts. The National Runaway Switchboard also found that LGBT youth are seven times more likely than their heterosexual homeless counterparts to be victims of crime.

Shelters Are Often Dangerous Places

Even when they seek help from social service agencies, however, not all LGBT youth are protected from being brutalized.

"For example," the report states, "in New York City, more than 60 percent of beds for homeless youth are provided by Covenant House, a facility where LGBT youth report that they have been threatened, belittled and abused by staff and other youth because of their sexual orientation or gender identity.

"At one residential placement facility in Michigan, LGBT teens, or those suspected of being LGBT, were forced to wear orange jumpsuits to alert staff and other residents," the summary continues. "At another transitional housing placement, staff removed the bedroom door of an out gay youth, supposedly to ward off any homosexual behavior. The second bed in the room was left empty and other residents were warned that if they misbehaved, they would have to share the room with the 'gay kid.'"

According to the report, "Many also said that the risks inherent to living in a space that was not protecting them made them think that they were better off having unsafe sex and contracting HIV, because they would then be eligible for specific housing funds reserved for HIV-positive homeless people."

Discrimination by Faith-Based Agencies

One of the problems, according to the agencies, is decreasing funding for homeless services and increasing funding for faith-based agencies, who are often antagonistic to LGBT youth.

"A number of faith-based providers oppose legal and social equality for LGBT people, which raises serious questions about whether LGBT homeless youth can access services in a safe and nurturing environment," Ray wrote. "For example, an internal Salvation Army document obtained by the *Washington Post* in 2001 confirmed that 'the White House had made a "firm commitment" to issue a regulation protecting religious charities from state and city efforts to prevent discrimination against gays in hiring and providing benefits.'"

Despite the bleakness of the overall report, the NGLTF and the NCH note five programs that could be models for outreach to LGBT homeless youth across the country. Two of them, Detroit's Ruth Ellis Center and Ann Arbor's Ozone House, are in Michigan, while Urban Peak in Denver, Green Chimneys in

A homeless transgender person prepares for the day at a lesbian, gay, bisexual, and transgender (LGBT) homeless shelter. Many in the LGBT homeless community are victims of family rejection because of their sexual orientation.

New York City and Waltham House in Massachusetts were also praised.

The document issues recommendations for helping the situation at the federal, state, local and service provider levels, including increasing funding for homeless youth services, developing a national estimate of homeless youth to aid in allocating resources, raising the minimum wage, dedicating specific shelter space to LGBT youth, expanding the availability of health insurance and requiring LGBT awareness training for licensed health and social service staff.

FOURTEEN

It Is Important
to Speak Out
About Homelessness

Cynthia Rae Eastman

The Reverend Cynthia Rae Eastman is a formerly homeless writer, activist, and founder of the humanitarian organizations Common Ground Worldwide and Earth Angel Volunteers, a knitting and crocheting group that makes caps, hats, scarves, gloves, and mittens for homeless/abused men, women, and children. In the following viewpoint Eastman argues that speaking out about homelessness can have a positive impact. She describes her experience of speaking up at a Homeless Services Oversight Council meeting in her community. After telling her own story of being a homeless mother of a thirteen-year-old, and how dangerous and frightening it was having to sleep in their car, the council decided to vote in favor of supporting safe parking for homeless people who are sleeping in their vehicles. The Reverend Eastman also gives a number of tips on how to make one's voice heard on the issue of homelessness.

Brianna [Karp] and I met a couple of years ago as authors writing for a blog on homelessness. Just like many of you reading "The Girl's Guide to Homelessness" blog [girlsguidetohomeless ness.com/blog], I too have been reading and watching her journey unfolding and morphing into what is now a book of the same title.

One thing that I have found to be extremely inspirational is the fact that in the midst of experiencing homelessness, Bri was always concerned about all of the others, who were suffering as a result of not being able to afford housing. From the very beginning, she was helping to serve as a voice for those who are homeless.

Clearly, she was thrust into positions of being interviewed on national television, which most of us will never experience. We could all tell that this was a bit scary for her, yet when opportunity knocked, despite the fear and unavoidable stigma associated with

Homeless individuals and their advocates hold a vigil for the homeless in Philadelphia. The author emphasizes the importance of speaking out for the less fortunate who, due to varying circumstances, have found themselves homeless.

Most States Lacking in Homeless Plans

A new report on child homelessness says a majority of states have inadequate plans to address the situation.

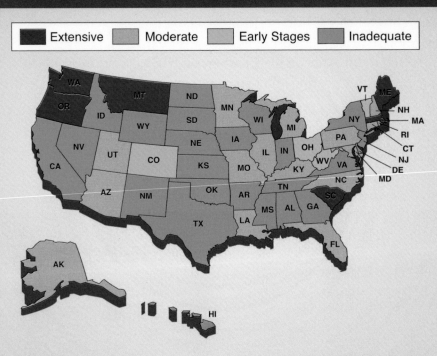

Policy and planning efforts grade

Extensive | Moderate | Early Stages | Inadequate

Taken from: The National Center on Family Homelessness. "Affordable Housing Initiatives," Trinity Foundation, 2008. www.trinityfi.org/housing.html.

being homeless, Bri courageously told her story and made sure that she did what she could to debunk the stereotypes.

Even though we may never personally be under that sort of spotlight, I would like to suggest that we have other smaller, yet powerful ways to have our voices heard. For example, recently, I was invited to speak at our local Homeless Services Oversight Council concerning giving a report on the National Conference on Ending Family Homelessness, which I attended in February. Following my presentation, I decided to remain for the rest of the meeting. During that time, the topic of creating a "Safe Parking" project came up.

Speaking Up Can Have a Positive Impact

As I listened, I could hear various members voicing concerns and the time came when, rather than voting on and passing their endorsement of this project, it looked like the item was going to be tabled in favor of more research. When the chairman of the council asked for "Citizen Comments," despite not planning to speak or having prepared anything to say, the sound of my tear-filled voice shocked even me.

"I was a divorced, single parent of a 13 year old, when I found myself between jobs," I said. Then continued with, "My son and I ended up sleeping in our car. It was terrifyingly dangerous. All night long the police kept telling us to move. In this county alone, there are over 3,800 men, women, and children, who are homeless and only 200 shelter beds. People MUST sleep somewhere! I just want to thank all of you for taking the steps necessary to help the people in our community, who are experiencing homelessness."

Much to my surprise, following these heartfelt impromptu words, a vote was again called and this time, it passed unanimously! It was the first time in my life that I realized my voice could have such a powerful impact and potentially make a positive change in the lives of others, who are struggling. After the meeting, the woman who was most opposed to moving forward with the vote came up to me and thanked me for putting a face to homelessness.

Tips for Having Your Voice Heard

- Write a letter to the editor of your local newspaper concerning something about which you feel passionate
- Create a blog and post your thoughts for change there. http://wordpress.org/ or www.b1ogger.com
- If you are currently homeless or have been un-housed in the past, join the "Faces of Homelessness" Speaker's Bureau [www.nationalhomeless.org/faces/index.html]

- For those of you who are service providers, start a "Faces of Homelessness" Speaker's Bureau [www.nationalhomeless. org/faces/setup.html]
- Join the World Homeless Action Movement on Facebook
- Attend the National Conference on Ending Homelessness [www.endhomelessness.org/content/calendar/detail/3692] (they offer amazing scholarships for folks who have experienced homelessness, which include transportation, hotel, registration, & a $75 stipend for misc. meals and ground transportation)

Most of all, I encourage you to remember this quote by Marianne Williamson [in her book *A Return to Love: Reflections on the Principles of "A Course of Miracles"*]:

Our deepest fear is not that we are inadequate. Our deepest fear is that we are powerful beyond measure. It is our light, not our darkness that most frightens us. We ask ourselves, "Who am I to be brilliant, gorgeous, talented, fabulous?" Actually, who are you not to be? You are a child of God. Your playing small does not serve the world. There's nothing enlightened about shrinking so that other people won't feel insecure around you. We are all meant to shine, as children do. We were born to make manifest the glory of God that is within us. It's not just in some of us; it's in everyone. And as we let our own light shine, we unconsciously give other people permission to do the same. As we're liberated from our own fear, our presence automatically liberates others.

It is critical for all of us to speak out in our communities concerning our experiences with homelessness. Our voices can be powerful tools for positive change. Let your light shine and your voice be heard, because one person truly can make a difference and that person is YOU!

FIFTEEN

A Homeless Teen Talks About Her Experience

Valencia McMurray

Valencia McMurray was one of fifty-five hundred homeless children counted by the Minneapolis Public Schools in 2008. She graduated from high school in 2009 and currently works as a writer while studying psychology at Augsburg College. In the following viewpoint McMurray describes her experience of being a homeless high school student, what led her into that situation, and how she got herself out of homelessness and into college.

I've been on my own since 10th grade, some months before my mom moved to Oklahoma to take care of my grandmother. My dad lives in Wisconsin and I don't exactly know him.

After my mom left, I shared an apartment with one of my four siblings in North Minneapolis. My brother and I both worked at Burger King to pay the rent.

A bunch of his friends moved in and next thing I knew, he lost his job and I was trying to support all these adults. I couldn't do it. This is where my homelessness began.

I ended up couch-hopping, staying at friends' places. I was missing a lot of school. My Advanced Placement U.S. History teacher Mr. Heegard could tell something was wrong.

"You would disappear for a week and I wouldn't know where you were. There was no way to get ahold of you. I started investigating. I don't think you were telling too many people," said Mr. Heegard.

I hadn't. I had trusted only two friends at school with my secret. One day after class, Mr. Heegard asked to see me. He asked what was going on. At first I said "nothing."

"You know, I think I had to tell you where you could go with your education. What you were capable of," said Mr. Heegard. "I knew it was just a matter of getting a break."

The school social worker found space for me at The Bridge, an emergency shelter for teens in South Minneapolis. I stayed there for three weeks before going to another shelter. For the last nine months I've been living in The Bridge's transitional housing program.

There are a lot of other kids in my situation.

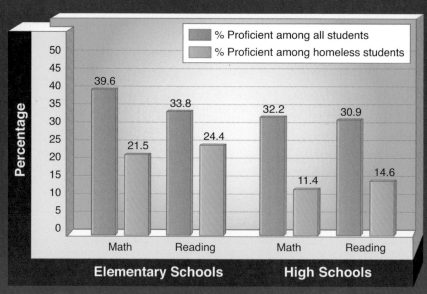

Academic Proficiency Among Homeless Students vs. All Students

Taken from: "Education of Homeless Children in America," *Campaign to End Child Homelessness*, The National Center on Family Homelessness, 2010. www.homelesschildrenamerica.org/findings_child-wellbeing_education.php?s=t.

Schoolwork Was Challenging

Elizabeth Hinz trains teachers and school staff—even custodians—in the Minneapolis Public Schools to be alert to signs of homelessness. She's the district liaison for homeless and highly mobile students.

I tell her at North High, I think my teachers did a pretty good job picking up on my situation. I was missing a lot of school. I wasn't really doing my homework as much as I was before and my grades were slipping.

"Some of the other clues are kids who are exhausted," said Hinz. "It might be wearing the same clothes a number of days in [a] row or looking disheveled. It might be being in the building but not in class, hanging out in [the] locker room or just some other quiet corner."

Hinz explains federal law requires public schools identify and educate homeless children. She shows me a chart of how homeless kids perform on standardized tests. Two-thirds are below grade-level. That's one of the impressions about homeless kids I'm out to disprove. Over the years, I've been in six Advanced Placement classes.

But it's been hard to keep myself motivated, to get up in the morning, to go to school and to do my homework.

When you're homeless, the only thing you have are endless days.

My friends and I come down to Hennepin Avenue where all the police hang out which is why I hate it. But there's a lot of stuff going on down here so I can't blame them. I got picked up on a curfew violation. I had to do community service raking leaves. It wasn't so bad.

I got in trouble again for curfew and ended up having to shovel snow. That was the worst. I would have rather raked some leaves.

Reading and Poetry

My favorite place to kill time is Barnes & Noble. They never kick you out. I used to try to talk my friends into going with me to Barnes & Noble so I could read, but they never wanted to go. They were always too loud. We'd end up leaving.

There are many programs in US cities that help homeless youths get an education.

All I have are words. I write poetry.

Mine to hold
A jungle made with my mind
A web
And I am the spider injecting venom into those who get
too close.
I get nervous and my fear makes me attack those who get
too near.
My fear
Is that my trusted words will be stolen.
I was made to share words,
But these words would crush the world that I'm holding.

I've never told a guy I've dated that I am homeless. They never ask. All I say is I don't live with my parents. That's what I tell people at school. I don't feel like that should be my opener when meeting people. Some people don't know how to deal with it.

I have a friend, a fellow poet, who also lives at The Bridge. I can't name her because of The Bridge's confidentiality rules. She says she's careful who she tells too.

"Nobody knows I am [homeless] unless I tell them," said my friend. "Just because you're from a certain place doesn't make you who you are. I'm not where I'm from, but where I'm from made me who I am."

We'll be leaving The Bridge this fall. We're both going to Augsburg College.

My efforts to stay in school paid off with a four-year scholarship. So for the next four years, I know where my home will be.

What You Should Know About Homelessness

Facts About Homelessness

According to the December 2010 United States Conference of Mayors's (USCM's) *Hunger and Homelessness Survey: A Status Report on Hunger and Homelessness in America's Cities: A 27-City Survey*:

- Severe mental disabilities affect about 24 percent of homeless adults.
- Physical disabilities affect 20 percent.
- Unemployment affects 81 percent.
- Domestic violence affects 14 percent.

The National Alliance to End Homelessness (NAEH) reports:

- About 77 percent of the US homeless population is found in completely urban areas, compared to 4 percent in completely rural areas.
- About one in four homeless people suffer from a serious mental illness such as bipolar disorder, schizophrenia, or chronic depression.
- Most single adult users of homeless shelters, about 80 percent, enter the shelter system only once or twice, remain for a little over a month, and never return.
- About 9 percent go into the shelter system around five times per year, stay almost two months each time, and use about 18 percent of the shelter's resources.

- The remaining approximately 10 percent go into the shelter system a couple of times a year, staying an average of 280 days each time; they essentially live in the shelter system and use up almost half of shelter resources.

According to NAEH's January 2011 *State of Homelessness in America* report:
- In 2009 approximately 656,129 people experienced homelessness on any given night, up from 636,234 in 2008—an increase of 3 percent.
- Of the homeless population, nearly two-thirds (412,973 out of 656,129) are individuals, with families (parents and their children) comprising the remaining 243,156.
- In 2008, 249,493 homeless people were unsheltered, increasing to 252,821 in 2009, an increase of 3,338 (1 percent).
- In 2008, 386,831 homeless people stayed in shelters, increasing to 403,308 in 2009.
- Homeless individuals (i.e., not members of families) numbered 399,420 in 2008; in 2009 homeless individuals numbered 412,973.
- In 2008 homeless veterans numbered an estimated 131,230 at any given time.
- The chronic or long-term homeless population was 111,323 in 2008, and in 2009 increased slightly to 112,076.

The National Coalition for Homeless Veterans reports:
- Veterans make up approximately 23 percent of the adult homeless and 20 percent of the total homeless population, despite being only 8 percent of the total US population.
- Approximately 95 percent of homeless veterans are men.
- About 56 percent of homeless veterans are Hispanic or African American, although they comprise only 12.8 percent and 15.4 percent, respectively, of the US general population.
- Of homeless veterans, 76 percent have mental health or substance abuse problems.

Homeless Families, Children, and Youth

According to Covenant House:

- Nearly 40 percent of the homeless population in the United States is under eighteen.
- Of homeless children, 57 percent go without food at least one day every month.
- Intense conflict or physical harm at the hands of a family member is cited by almost 50 percent of homeless youth as a major factor contributing to their homelessness. More than 25 percent of former foster children experience homelessness two to four years after leaving the foster care system.
- Half of teens too old to stay in the foster care or juvenile justice systems become homeless in less than six months due to limited education, a lack of social support, and being unprepared to live on their own.

Among children helped by Covenant House:

- 41 percent saw acts of violence in their homes.
- 36 percent reported that someone in their family regularly used drugs.
- 19 percent indicated that they had been beaten with an object.
- 19 percent had experienced sexual abuse.
- 15 percent said someone close to them had been murdered.

According to the NAEH:

- Long-term homelessness is experienced by an estimated 50,000 US youth.
- Approximately 13 percent of homeless families say they left their last home because of violence or abuse.
- In 2008 homeless persons in families numbered 236,904; in 2009 this number increased 3 percent, to 243,156.
- Young adults aging out of foster care (i.e., they are too old to stay in the foster care system) have an estimated one in six chance of homelessness over the course of a year. In both 2008 and 2009 about 29,500 youth aged out of foster care.

The American Psychological Association (APA) reports:

- School districts surveyed in fall 2008 said that the number of homeless students had increased due to the recession; this followed increases in 2006 and 2007.
- Among homeless youth, family conflict is the main cause of homelessness; 46 percent report abuse.
- Estimates of homeless youth who identify as gay, lesbian, bisexual, or transgender range from 20 to 40 percent.
- Of children in the United States, one in fifty, or 1.5 million children, is estimated to be homeless, with 650,000 below the age of six.
- Over one-third of homeless single mothers suffer from post-traumatic stress disorder (PTSD).
- More than half of homeless single mothers have experienced major depression, and about 41 percent have been dependent on alcohol or other drugs.

Causes of Homelessness

According to NAEH's January 2011 *State of Homelessness in America* report:

- In 2008, 5,398,379 American households experienced a severe housing cost burden (paying more than 50 percent of income on rent), rising in 2009 to 5,886,293—an increase of 9 percent.
- Lack of a job is a commonly given reason for homelessness. In 2008, 8,924,000 individuals in the United States were unemployed, rising to 14,265,000 in 2009—an increase of 59.9 percent.
- In 2008, 2,330,483 housing units in the United States were in foreclosure, rising to 2,824,674 in 2009, an increase of 21.2 percent.
- Those who are "doubled up"—that is, living with family or friends because of economic hardship—have a one in ten chance of being homeless at some point in a given year. From 2008 to 2009 the number of doubled-up people in the United States increased from 5,402,075 to 6,037,256, an increase of 12 percent.

- People being discharged from prison have a one in eleven chance of homelessness over a given year. Between 2007 and 2008 the number of discharged prisoners increased from 669,194 to 679,738, an increase of 2 percent.
- Those lacking health insurance are considered to have a greater risk of homelessness than those with insurance coverage. In 2008, there were 46,728,637 uninsured people in the United States; in 2009, the number increased by 1 percent to 47,151,404—an increase of 422,767 people.

According to USCM's December 2010 *Hunger and Homelessness Survey: A Status Report on Hunger and Homelessness in America's Cities: A 27-City Survey:*

In identifying the three main causes of homelessness among families with children in the cities surveyed,
- 76 percent referred to unemployment;
- 72 percent referred to lack of affordable housing;
- 56 percent referred to poverty;
- 24 percent referred to domestic violence; and
- 20 percent referred to low-paying jobs.

In identifying the three main causes of homelessness among individuals,
- 31 percent referred to lack of affordable housing;
- 19 percent referred to mental illness combined with a lack of necessary services;
- 19 percent referred to substance abuse combined with a lack of services; and
- 15 percent referred to poverty.

Consequences of Homelessness

The NAEH reports:
- A *New England Journal of Medicine* report found that homeless individuals stayed in a hospital about four days longer each visit than the non-homeless, resulting in an additional cost of $2,414 per hospitalization.

- A Hawaii study of hospital admissions found that 1,751 homeless adults had 564 hospital visits, at a total cost of $4 million.
- The homeless also had a rate of psychiatric hospitalization more than one hundred times higher than the non-homeless population.
- Homeless people are in jail or prison more often than the general population, often for crimes such as begging, sleeping in cars, and loitering. Typically, a prison bed in a federal or state prison costs about $20,000 a year.
- A University of Texas study of homeless individuals over a two-year period found that on average each cost taxpayers $14,480, mostly for overnight jail.

According to Up With Women, reporting on a study done in Toronto, Ontario, Canada:
- Whereas 2 percent of the general population reported experiencing traffic-related injuries as pedestrians, the rate among the homeless population was 11.4 percent.
- Of homeless women, 43.3 percent had experienced assault or sexual harassment in the previous year.
- Whereas 16 percent of the general population reported experiencing fatigue in the previous month, among the homeless the rate was 43 percent.
- Half of the homeless people studied said they had less than six hours of sleep during four or more nights of the previous week.
- Of the homeless studied, 26.8 percent had thought about suicide in the previous year.
- Of the homeless studied, 7.8 percent had attempted suicide in the previous year.
- Half of those studied indicated that they did not know anyone who could help them during an emotional crisis they could not deal with on their own.

The APA reports:
- Homeless children lack needed stability in their lives, with 97 percent moving at least once per year.

- Of homeless children, 22 percent have been separated from their families.
- Homeless children are twice as likely to go hungry than non-homeless children.
- Homelessness is associated with poor physical health for children, including malnutrition, low birth weight, exposure to toxins, and long-term illnesses such as asthma.
- Compared to the general population, homeless children are twice as likely to have repeated a grade in school, been suspended from school, or to have a learning disability.
- About one in four homeless children have witnessed violence.
- Depression and anxiety affects half of homeless children of school age. One in five homeless preschool children has emotional problems serious enough to require professional care.

Challenges and Successes in Dealing with Homelessness

According to USCM's December 2010 *Hunger and Homelessness Survey: A Status Report on Hunger and Homelessness in America's Cities: A 27-City Survey:*

- In 71 percent of the cities surveyed, clients of homeless shelters often have to sleep in chairs, hallways, or have other inadequate sleeping arrangements because not enough beds are available.
- In 64 percent of cities, emergency shelters have had to turn away homeless individuals because no beds were available.
- In 68 percent of surveyed cities, shelters have had to turn away homeless families with children, due to unavailability of beds.
- City officials estimate that 27 percent of those in need of assistance do not get the help they need.
- Of cities surveyed, 92 percent indicated a need for more assisted housing resources for the homeless.
- 83 percent indicated a need for more supportive housing for homeless people with disabilities.

- 71 percent indicated a need for more and better-paying jobs.
- 37.5 percent indicated a need for increased substance-abuse resources.

The NAEH reports:
- Portland, Oregon, reported that each of thirty-five chronically homeless people used more than $42,000 in public resources each year; after being given permanent supportive housing as part of the Community Engagement Program, each used less than $26,000 a year (including the cost of housing), thus saving more than $16,000 per person.
- In Seattle, Washington, a study found a cost savings of over 50 percent among homeless people given permanent supportive housing, amounting to a savings of over $30,000 per person per year.
- Portland, Maine, after giving chronically homeless people permanent supportive housing, found that it saved $1,296 per person in emergency room costs each year.
- When San Francisco, California, gave chronically homeless individuals permanent supportive housing, emergency department costs for serving the chronically homeless dropped by 56 percent.
- A study in Los Angeles, California, where 10 percent of the entire US homeless population lives, revealed that the city saved $80,000 per year by giving permanent supportive housing to four chronically homeless individuals.

What You Should Do About Homelessness

Gather Information

The first step in grappling with any complex and controversial issue is to be informed about it. Gather as much information as you can from a variety of sources. The essays in this book form an excellent starting point, representing a variety of viewpoints and approaches to the topic. Your school or local library will be another source of useful information; look there for relevant books, magazines, and encyclopedia entries. The Bibliography and Organizations to Contact sections of this book will give you useful starting points in gathering additional information.

Ever since the United Nations declared 1987 the International Year of Shelter for the Homeless, there has been ever increasing interest in the problem of homelessness. Numerous organizations address the problem both in the United States and around the world and can provide information and perspectives on homelessness and proposed solutions. Many articles, books, and other resources that deal with the topic have been published in recent years. As well, academic papers (e.g., sociological studies) on homelessness are available. If the information in such a paper is too dense or technical, check the abstract at the beginning of the article. The abstract provides a clear summary of the researcher's conclusions.

You may also want to find and interview people who have experienced homelessness or who have worked with the homeless. Most areas have organizations that help the homeless; such groups can be contacted by phone or via the Internet (start with the Organizations to Contact section of this book).

Identify the Issues Involved

Once you have gathered your information, review it methodically to discover the key issues involved. What theories do people have about the causes of homelessness? How prevalent is homelessness? Who is affected by homelessness? Are there certain factors that are associated with homelessness, such as poverty, drug addiction, mental or physical illness, sexual or physical abuse? How does the state of the economy at a given time influence homelessness? What programs are available or proposed to deal with homelessness, and how successful have they been? Have ideas about homelessness or how to treat it changed over time? To get a broader perspective on what is happening in America today, it may be worthwhile to consider how homelessness has shown up in other cultures and time periods.

You may find that approaches to dealing with homelessness vary depending on the beliefs of the people or agencies involved. For example, some consider homelessness to be the result of factors such as poverty or inadequate health care and may favor social support systems designed to help those in need. Others may consider homelessness to be a chosen lifestyle or the result of character flaws and may favor a "tough love" approach or doing nothing at all. Those with a spiritual orientation may want to help the homeless to find faith in a higher power, and so on.

Evaluate Your Information Sources

In developing your own opinion, it is vital to evaluate the sources of the information you have discovered. Authors of books, magazine articles, etc., however well-intentioned, have their own perspectives and biases that may affect how they present information on the subject. Homelessness is a controversial and complicated issue, and people have different ways of looking at it.

Consider the authors' credentials and what organizations they are affiliated with. For example, an article written by a social activist may focus on factors such as the high cost of housing or unequal distribution of wealth in the United States. An article written by a psychologist, on the other hand, might focus on mental health issues among the chronically homeless. Both articles may offer valid information, but each will present data that support its author's viewpoint and that of the organizations the author is associated with. Critically evaluate and assess your sources rather than take whatever they say at face value.

Examine Your Own Perspective

Homelessness is a complex and emotionally charged topic. Spend some time exploring your own thoughts and feelings about homelessness. Consider the attitudes and beliefs on this issue that you have received from family members, friends, and the media throughout your life. Such messages affect your own thoughts and feelings about the subject. Have you or anyone you know ever experienced homelessness? Schools report an increasing number of homeless students, many of whom do their best to conceal their homelessness. Consider how you might feel if you discovered a friend of yours was secretly homeless. If you became homeless, how would you feel? What would you do? If you or someone close to you has experienced homelessness, you may find it challenging to form a clear view of the issues involved, or you might have special insight into the topic.

Form Your Own Opinion and Take Action

Once you have gathered and organized information, identified the issues involved, and examined your own perspective, you will be ready to form an opinion on homelessness and to advocate your position in debates and discussions (and if you or someone close to you is experiencing homelessness, you will have a better idea of what resources are available and what approaches to take to deal with the problem). Perhaps you will conclude that one of the viewpoints you have encountered offers the best explanation of what causes homelessness and how to deal with it, or you may decide that a number of approaches working together are needed to adequately address this complex issue. You might even decide that none of the perspectives on homelessness that you have encountered are convincing to you and that you cannot take a decisive position yet. If that is the case, ask yourself what you would need to know to make up your mind; perhaps a bit more research would be helpful. Whatever position you take, be prepared to explain it clearly based on facts, evidence, and well-thought-out beliefs.

ORGANIZATIONS TO CONTACT

The editors have compiled the following list of organizations concerned with the issues debated in this book. The descriptions are derived from materials provided by the organizations. All have publications or information available for interested readers. The list was compiled on the date of publication of the present volume; the information provided here may change. Be aware that many organizations take several weeks or longer to respond to inquiries, so allow as much time as possible for the receipt of requested materials.

Administration for Children and Families (ACF)
US Department of Health and Human Services
370 L'Enfant Promenade SW, Washington, DC 20447
(202) 205-8102 • fax: (202) 260-9333
website: www.acf.hhs.gov

The ACF, within the Department of Health and Human Services (HHS), is responsible for federal programs that promote the economic and social well-being of families, children, individuals, and communities. Target populations include runaway and homeless youth, victims of family violence, children of prisoners, and youth at risk for early sexual activity. The website features posters, brochures, fact sheets, research reports, and links to other agencies.

Children of the Night
14530 Sylvan St., Van Nuys, CA 91411
(818) 908-4474
help hotline (toll free): (800) 551-1300 • fax: (818) 908-1468
e-mail: llee@childrenofthenight.org
website: www.childrenofthenight.org

Children of the Night is a private organization founded in 1979. It is dedicated to assisting children between the ages of eleven and seventeen who are forced to prostitute on the streets for food to eat and a place to sleep. The group works with detectives, FBI agents, and prosecutors in cities including Los Angeles, Hollywood, Las Vegas, Seattle, Miami, New York, Minneapolis, Atlanta, Phoenix, Hawaii, and Washington, D.C., and provides a twenty-four-hour-a-day hotline serviced by trained staff who can help teens find shelter, counseling, and protection.

Child Welfare League of America (CWLA)

2345 Crystal Dr., Ste. 250, Arlington, VA 22202
(703) 412-2400 • fax: (703) 412-2401
website: www.cwla.org

CWLA is an association of nearly eight hundred public and private nonprofit agencies that assist more than 3.5 million abused and neglected children and their families each year with a range of services. The league also works through advocacy and education to shape public policy regarding the welfare of children, and conducts research to determine and disseminate best practices for professionals and volunteers working with children. Its website offers press releases, research results, and descriptions of programs. Of particular interest is the section Practice Areas: Housing and Homelessness, which provides a number of publications and reports, including *The Child Protection–Housing Connection*, *Programs and Resources for Youth Aging Out of Foster Care*, and *USG Positive Parenting Program for Homeless Families: Implementation Guide*.

Committee on the Shelterless (COTS)

PO Box 2744, Petaluma, CA 94953
(707) 765-6530 • website: www.cots-homeless.org

COTS was founded in 1988 as an expression of Mary Isaak's and Laure Reichek's concern for children and adults who were sleeping outdoors in culverts, dumpsters, or other unsafe and unsuitable conditions. Its mission is to help homeless families become stable and break the cycle of homelessness by teaching homeless parents to make their children's needs a high priority and to provide a safe, loving, and secure home for their children. Each year COTS volunteers donate over fifty thousand hours to help the homeless population in Sonoma County, California. Its website offers a variety of information on its program for comprehensively addressing the problems associated with homelessness; see the heading "How We Help" for more on this program. The organization also published the book *Invitation to Service: Stories from COTS*.

Covenant House
Times Square Station, New York, NY 10108-0900
(800) 999-9999 • website: www.covenanthouse.org

Covenant House is the largest privately funded nonprofit agency in North and Central America providing shelter and other services to homeless, runaway, and throwaway youth. Its NINELINE crisis hotline, (800) 999-9999, takes free and confidential phone calls from young people in crisis. The NINELINE is also available on the Internet at www.NINELINE.org, where young people can submit questions via e-mail or participate in forum conversations monitored by NINELINE counselors. Incorporated in New York City in 1972, Covenant House International has facilities in twenty-one cities throughout the United States, Canada, Guatemala, Honduras, Mexico, and Nicaragua. Its website offers information for prospective advocates and volunteers, as well as a link to its newsletter *The Covenant House Beacon*.

Habitat for Humanity International
121 Habitat St., Americus, GA 31709-3498
(800) 422-4828
e-mail: youthprograms@habitat.org • website: www.habitat.org

Habitat for Humanity is a nonprofit, ecumenical Christian ministry that believes that every man, woman, and child should have a decent, safe, and affordable place to live. The organization helps to construct houses for some of the nearly 100 million homeless people around the world, as well as the nearly 2 billion people who live in slum housing. Its website offers a variety of information on its projects. Of special interest is the section "Habitat Youth Programs" (www.habitat.org/youthprograms), which offers a variety of ways that youth can get involved.

National Alliance to End Homelessness

1518 K St. NW, Ste. 410, Washington, DC 20005
(202) 638-1526 • fax: (202) 638-4664
e-mail: naeh@naeh.org • website: www.endhomelessness.org

The National Alliance to End Homelessness, founded in 1983, is a nonprofit organization committed to preventing and ending homelessness in the United States. The alliance works with the public, private, and nonprofit sectors to create stronger programs and policies that help communities achieve their goal of ending homelessness, and provide data and research on homelessness to policy makers and elected officials. Its website offers a wealth of information on all aspects of homelessness.

National Coalition for Homeless Veterans

333 ½ Pennsylvania Ave. SE, Washington, DC 20003-1148
(202) 546-1969 or (800) 838-4357
fax: (202) 546-2063 or (888) 233-8582
e-mail: info@nchv.org • website: www.nchv.org

The National Coalition for Homeless Veterans is the resource and technical assistance center for a national network of community-based service providers and local, state, and federal agencies that provide emergency and supportive housing, food, health services, job training and placement assistance, legal aid, and case management support for hundreds of thousands of homeless veterans each year. Its website offers a variety of information and resources dealing with veteran homelessness. Publications include brochures and fact sheets, the monthly *NCHV e-Newsletter*, and information guides.

National Coalition for the Homeless

2201 P St. NW, Washington, DC 20037
(202) 462-4822 • fax: (202) 462-4823
e-mail: info@nationalhomeless.org
website: www.nationalhomeless.org

The National Coalition for the Homeless, founded in 1981, is a national network of people who are currently experiencing or who have experienced homelessness, activists and advocates, community-based and faith-based service providers, and others committed to end homelessness. The organization works to meet the immediate needs of people who are currently experiencing homelessness or who are at risk of doing so. It also engages in public education and grassroots organizing, and it advocates for changes in public policy toward homelessness. The organization's website offers fact sheets, a variety of publications and reports, and a monthly newsletter (archived copies of which can be found in the Publications section). Under the Directories heading are lists of other national and local organizations to help the homeless.

National Network for Youth (NN4Y)
741 Eighth St. SE, Washington, DC 20003
(202) 783-7949 • website: www.nn4youth.org

The NN4Y serves the needs of runaway, homeless, and other disconnected youth through a network of community-based organizations. The organization's website offers a Youth Referral and Information Resources Directory as well as a free e-newsletter, *NN4Y ENews*. It also runs a national crisis hotline for runaway youth (1-800-RUNAWAY) and associated website (www.1800runaway.org).

National Student Campaign Against Hunger and Homelessness
National Organizing Office
328 S. Jefferson St., Ste. 620, Chicago, IL 60605
(312) 544-4436 (ext. 204) • fax: (312) 275-7150
e-mail: info@studentsagainsthunger.org
website: www.studentsagainsthunger.org

Founded in 1985 by state Public Interest Research Groups (PIRGs), the campaign is committed to ending hunger and homelessness in America by educating, engaging, and training high school and college students to directly meet individuals' immediate needs while advocating for long-term systemic solutions. The organization offers training materials and fact sheets, information about hunger and homelessness, and opportunities for volunteers.

StandUp for Kids
83 Walton St., Ste. 100, Atlanta, GA 30303
(800) 365-4543 • fax: (404) 954-6610

e-mail: staff@standupforkids.org
website: www.standupforkids.org

The mission of StandUp for Kids, an independent organization founded in 1990, is to help homeless and street people aged twenty-one and younger. Volunteers in dozens of states and Washington, D.C., identify, befriend, and support young people living in the streets, and work with schools and through the Internet to help young people find ways to stay off the street. The website provides short videos, statistical information, and a link to subscribe to the *StandUp for Kids* monthly newsletter.

Up With Women

800 W First St., Ste. 1607, Los Angeles, CA 90012-2424
e-mail: lia@upwithwomen.com • website: www.upwithwomen.com

Up With Women was founded to challenge the stereotypes of homelessness and to help homeless women and children in the United States and Canada to rebuild their lives. It aims to help get women out of abusive homes, off the streets, out of shelters, and into safe, permanent housing with the financial stability to support themselves and their families. Its website offers facts about homelessness, inspiring success stories, and audio and video clips. The organization also funds support programs for housing, safety, and the economic empowerment of women.

Volunteers of America

1660 Duke St., Alexandria, VA 22314
(703) 341-5000 or (800) 899-0089 • fax: (703) 341-7000
e-mail: volunteers@voa.org • website: www.voa.org

Volunteers of America is a nonprofit organization comprised of nearly sixteen thousand paid, professional employees, and sixty-five thousand volunteers, dedicated to helping those in need rebuild their lives and reach their full potential. The organization's homelessness section (www.voa.org/Get-Help/National-Network-of-Services/Homelessness) offers information on emergency shelter, outreach programs, drop-in centers, and other supportive services designed to help homeless individuals and families.

BIBLIOGRAPHY

Books

Lynn Blodgett and Laurie Kratochvil, *Finding Grace: The Face of America's Homeless*. San Rafael, CA: Earth Aware, 2007.

Cadillac Man, *Land of the Lost Souls: My Life on the Streets*. New York: Bloomsbury, 2009.

William G. Connell, *Homeless in Paradise: Communicating with the Bohemian Venice Beach, CA Sub-Culture*. Raleigh, NC: Lulu, 2008.

Janice Erlbaum, *Girlbomb: A Halfway Homeless Memoir*. New York: Villard, 2007.

Janice Erlbaum, *Have You Found Her: A Memoir*. New York: Villard, 2008.

R. Barri Flowers, *Street Kids: The Lives of Runaway and Thrownaway Teens*. Jefferson, NC: McFarland, 2010.

Ron Hall, Denver Moore, and Lynn Vincent, *Same Kind of Different as Me*. Nashville: Thomas Nelson, 2006.

Kevin D. Hendricks, *Open Our Eyes: Seeing the Invisible People of Homelessness*. St. Paul, MN: Monkey Outta Nowhere, 2010.

Jonathan Kozol, *Rachel and Her Children: Homeless Families in America*. New York: Three Rivers, 2006.

Susan Madden Lankford, *DownTown U.S.A.: A Personal Journey with the Homeless*. San Diego: Human Exposures, 2009.

Richard LeMieux, *Breakfast at Sally's: One Homeless Man's Inspirational Journey*. New York: Skyhorse, 2008.

Steve Lopez, *The Soloist: A Lost Dream, an Unlikely Friendship, and the Redemptive Power of Music*. New York: G.P. Putnam's Sons, 2008.

Liz Murray, *Breaking Night: A Memoir of Forgiveness, Survival, and My Journey from Homeless to Harvard*. New York: Hyperion, 2010.

Michael Oher, with Don Yaeger, *I Beat the Odds: From Homelessness, to the Blind Side, and Beyond*. New York: Gotham, 2011.

John Records, *Invitation to Service: Stories from COTS*. Petaluma, CA: Friends of COTS, 2008.

Adam Shepard, *Scratch Beginnings: Me, $25, and the Search for the American Dream*. New York: Collins, 2008.

Teun Voeten, *Tunnel People*. Oakland: PM, 2010.

Tom Waits and Michael Brien, *Hard Ground*, Austin: University of Texas Press, 2011.

Periodicals and Internet Sources

Sharon Abercrombie, "Faithful Fools Chip Away at the Boundaries; Franciscan Nun Teams with Unitarian Minister to Serve in San Francisco's Tenderloin District." *National Catholic Reporter*, February 20, 2009.

Marisa Agha, "Transition to Civilian Life Challenging for Homeless Female Veterans," *Sacramento Bee*, March 6, 2011. www.sacbee .com/2011/03/06/3452876/transition-to-civilian-life-challenging .html.

Becky Blanton, "What We Talk About When We Talk About Homelessness," change.org, May 13, 2010. http://news.change .org/stories/what-we-talk-about-when-we-talk-about-homeless ness.

Meredith Bolster, "Myths About the Homeless," part 1, *Bangor Daily News*, April 1, 2011. http://bangordailynews .com/2011/04/01/health/myths-about-homelessness.

———, "Myths About the Homeless," part 2, *Bangor Daily News*, April 8, 2011. http://bangordailynews.com/2011/04/08/health/ myths-about-the-homeless-part-2.

Jason Cherkis, "Obama Administration Seeks to Address Homeless Crisis Among Gay Teens," *Huffington Post*, June 1, 2011. www .huffingtonpost.com/2011/06/01/obama-administration-gay-teens-homeless-crisis_n_869901.html.

Ian Chillag, "Running from Trouble," *Runner's World*, February 2009. www.runnersworld.com/article/0,7120,s6-243-297 --13022-1-1X2X3X4X5X6X7X8X9-9,00.html.

Andrew Denney and Catherine Martin, "Helping the Homeless," *Columbia Daily Tribune*, March 6, 2011. www.columbiatribune. com/news/2011/mar/06/helping-the-homeless.

Emmy Dworkin, "Tiny Casualties: Fighting Childhood Homelessness Is an Uphill Battle," *Celeb Life Magazine*, Spring 2008.

Maco L. Faniel, "Black Face—The Minstrel Show of Homelessness," *Regal Magazine*, December 10, 2009. www.regalmag.com/urban -homelessness-black-face-a-419.html.

Maria Foscarinis, "U.S. Should Uphold Homeless Promises to U.N.," *Huffington Post*, March 19, 2011. www.huffingtonpost .com/maria-foscarinis/us--homelessness-human-rights_b_837150 .html.

Gary Horton, "It Could Be Any of Us," *Signal*, April 6, 2001. www .the-signal.com/archives/42953.

Mark Horvath, "My First Night Homeless," Change.org, January 5, 2009. http://news.change.org/stories/my-first-night-homeless.

Institute of Noetic Sciences, "Personal Growth Program Guides Homeless Adults to Self-Sufficiency by Repairing Inner Resources," September 2010. www.noetic.org/about/case-studies/ home.

Gina Kim, "Safe Ground Offers Strength in Numbers, but Its Homeless Must Move Often," *Sacramento Bee*, March 5, 2011. www.sacbee.com/2011/03/05/3451201/safe-ground-offers -strength-in.html.

Robert Kolker, "A Night on the Streets: Homelessness Is the Single Biggest Failure of the Bloomberg Administration, Which Has Tried a Radical New Policy That's Made an Intractable Problem Worse. There Are Over 35,000 Homeless Now in the City. On a Single Cold Night in February, We Met Six of Them," *New York Magazine*, March 17, 2008.

Nicolas D. Kristof, "What Could You Live Without?," *New York Times*, January 23, 2010. www.nytimes.com/2010/01/24/opinion/24kristof.html.

Stephen M. Lilienthal, "The Problem Is Not the Homeless," *Library Journal*, July 23, 2011. www.libraryjournal.com/lj/home/890752-264/the_problem_is_not_the.html.csp.

Jean Marbella, "Homeless, Out of Work, but Not Hopeless." *Baltimore Sun*, March 1, 2009. http://articles.baltimoresun.com/2009-03-01/news/0902270086_1_homeless-shelter-ending-homelessness-prevent-homelessness.

Lisa Pemberton, "Student Homelessness Tests Families, Schools," *Tacoma (WA) News Tribune*, April 3, 2011. www.thenewstribune.com/2011/04/03/1610713/student-homelessness-tests-families.html.

Stephen Rodrick, "Spartan Warriors in the YouTube Age. Or, the Legend of Legend, Spider, and Science; in Union Square, a Gang of Enterprising, Mostly Homeless Youths Are Pummeling Each Other for Your Amusement, a Few Bucks, and Hopes of Immortality," *New York Magazine*, July 28, 2008.

Paul Schott, "Not Homeless but 'Free,' Man Chooses to Endure the Elements," *Danbury (CT) News-Times*, March 6, 2011. www.newstimes.com/local/article/Not-homeless-but-free-man-chooses-to-endure-1045301.php.

Science Daily, "Archeology of Homelessness," November 26, 2008. www.sciencedaily.com/releases/2008/11/081124130956.htm.

Amy Taylor, "Abstinence Not Necessary," *Community Care*, August 21, 2009. www.communitycare.co.uk/Articles/2009/08/21/112415/St-Mungo39s-LifeWorks-psychotherapy-scheme.htm.

Anita Valentin, "Divine Inspiration: Cafe Serves Up Job Training, with Extra Miracles on the Side," *Chicago Reporter*, July/August 2008.

Mary Vorsino, "Parents Raise Tots in Tents Rather than Go to Shelters," *Honolulu Star-Advertiser*, April 3, 2011. www.staradvertiser.com/news/20110403_Parents_raise_tots_in_tents_rather_than_go_to_shelters.html.

Misha Warbanski, "Homeless at 40 Below," *Herizons*, Winter 2009.

Richard A. Webster, "The Invisible Population: Homeless People Living in New Orleans–Area Blighted Buildings," *New Orleans City Business*, 2009.

Rachael Whitcomb, "Helping Hands: Florida Veterinarian Visits Homeless Camps to Care for Pets, Finds Service Rewarding," *DVM Newsmagazine*, vol. 40, no. 7, 2009.

Elaine Zablocki, "Community Care: Help Patients Fulfill Basic Needs, and They Can Better Attend to Their Healthcare," *Managed Healthcare Executive*, vol. 19, no. 8, 2009.

Gregg Zoroya, "Recent War Vets Face Risk of Homelessness," *USA Today*, July 26, 2011. www.usatoday.com/news/military/2011-07-25-homeless-veterans_n.htm.